Octavio Paz
Early Poems
1935-1955

"The growth of the work of Octavio Paz," writes Muriel Rukeyser in her preface to this bilingual selection of the Mexican poet's Early Poems, "has made clear to an audience in many languages what was evident from the beginning . . . he is a great poet, a world-poet whom we need. The poems here speak—as does all his work since—deeply, erotically, with grave and passionate involvement."

In this, a much revised edition of the earlier *Selected Poems*, Miss Rukeyser has joined to her own translations those of Paul Blackburn, Lysander Kemp, Denise Levertov, and William Carlos Williams, while many of the readings embody Paz's own revisions of the original texts.

The poetry of Paz bears witness to two influences: the native Mexican and the Spanish-European. Images abound from Mexico's Indian past and her colorful contemporary life and landscape; striking portraits bring to life moments from his country's history which are then related to the modern scene. Often revealing a suppressed violence, ⬚⬚⬚⬚ ⬚⬚⬚⬚⬚ bear the stamp of the c⬚⬚⬚ and diplomat.

EARLY POEMS 1935–1955

Also by Octavio Paz

Configurations

Octavio Paz

EARLY POEMS 1935–1955

Translated from the Spanish by MURIEL RUKEYSER and other poets,
including PAUL BLACKBURN, LYSANDER KEMP, DENISE LEVERTOV,
and WILLIAM CARLOS WILLIAMS

Indiana University Press
Bloomington and London

Cloth edition published in 1973 by Indiana University Press.

UNESCO Collection of Representative Works. This book has been accepted in the
Latin American Series of the Translations Collection of the United Nations Educational,
Scientific and Cultural Organization (UNESCO).

Grateful acknowledgement is made to the Fondo de Cultura Economica for permission
to reprint the Spanish text of poems from the volume *Libertad bajo palabra ; obra poetica*
by Octavio Paz (Mexico, D.F., 1960).

Published in Canada by Fitzhenry & Whiteside Limited, Don Mills, Ontario
Library of Congress catalog card number: 72-93981
ISBN: 0-253-31867-X
Manufactured in the United States of America

FOREWORD—1963 Edition

In coming to the poems of the young Octavio Paz, I found that voice of the meeting-place for which many of us were looking in those years. Meeting-place of fever and the cold eye, in a passion which could hold together with his own arms the flying apart of his own time. He claimed it, its past and the moment that held it with its own arms, the present. They were lyrics he brought to me, cut as if with an adze; and I began to translate.

In his early lyrics, with their speed, their transparencies, their couples lying together, all couples, all opposites, there was a chance for the reader to see what was flashing out of Mexico in this young poet. He glittered in his airs and silences, his sudden strokes:

> Our bones are lightning
> in the night of the flesh.
> O world, all is night,
> life is the lightning.

These were in a book called *Condición de nube*; and now I was double reader, for I was beginning to translate, and what is that title? It is like bringing over the French term *réalité*. What is that *condición*, that reminds us of the human condition? The word *level* has been turned into sheer shaking naught, in our language; *phase* is closer, and expressed what Paz was beginning to express, the sense of transformation which I have been valuing in my writing, in all writing.

It meant very much to me to begin to bring over the poems he had shown me, in Berkeley, in 1944. But it was only the beginning of a long involvement with this work, which for me has opened and changed and sometimes shut altogether, never to go on, it appeared then; and after that has itself transformed, transforming me, as any work transforms the doer, but as great work deeply transforms all it touches.

Perhaps recounting the stages of accomplishing this book will tell you something of the nature of this poet.

By the time I had published the first group of translations and come to the next poems—poems that ranged much farther, that grew and went deep into the inner life and the old life, Nahuatl as well as Mexican—I was going back over the translations, seeing where I had stumbled in

bringing them over into English. I wanted them to come through, as they could, in poetry for this language. This second group out of *Semillas para un himno*, went beyond what M. L. Rosenthal has called Paz's 'literal statement of consciousness, very delicate and exact' which spoke from his early poetry. Here he is the master; he is engaged in his task.

'He has come to his task,' J. M. Cohen writes of Paz in *Poetry of this Age* (London: Grey Arrow, 1959), 'by way of a persistent questioning of all reality.' The questioning leads him again to phases, to transformations, in which land approaches the state of sculpture,

> The naked forehead of the world is raised
> Rock smoothed and polished to cut a poem on
> Display of light that opens its fan of names
> Here is the seed of a singing like a tree

and this world opens its burning men and women. In another poem, 'In her splendor islanded,'*

> She is lake-water in April as she lies
> In her depths binding poplar and eucalyptus
> Fishes or stars burning between her thighs
> Shadows of birds scarcely hiding her sex

Octavio Paz had come, before this time, out of his student frenzy, out of the fighting grief, the grief buried of the civil war in Spain, which gave him his 'Elegy for a friend,' and to the great world of these transformed, the world in which he has always lived, moving in transformation among the inner life and the life of the interchange of people in politics and communication. In the posts in the Mexican diplomatic service, in the United Nations, in the embassies in Paris and in New Delhi—where he now is—he moves as the poet who has spoken as much as anyone of his time for the assertion of hope and the assertion of despair, in a war to the death of both, in a war that will kill all images and then, with a movement that is of necessity religious, transform all images.

'Paz seems to have set out in search of the most desperate experience in order to emerge from it with at least a grain of hope,' says Ramon Xirau, the Mexican whose writing about Paz is brilliant and in deepest sympathy: Paz and Xirau draw strength from the same sources.

As translator I was compelled to these sources: pain as speech, trust in the ancient—not as sacrifice, but as trust, to cut out one's heart in order to feed the sun, to face the cycle because you know it is the only way through and *it turns*, it is you who are brought through. As you are in coming to a work of art, your own or another's whose images you go

* Not in present edition.

deeper and deeper with; you know that however you emerge, it will be with different desires.

I came then to *Piedra de Sol*,* the long marvelous poem of the changes for which the Sun Stone, the Mexican Calendar Stone, stands. It is really an anima poem in the Jungian sense, going through the changes of the world as woman and opposite; it goes to the root of experience in the instant, by declaring the eternal there; in love, by declaring the Other there; in experience, by finding the Otherwise there; and meeting the self absorbed, the world absorbed, at every place in the dance. The poem of these changes has been published separately, but here, in Octavio Paz's own choice for his *Selected Poems*, the reader can follow the same journey. It is the journey of the poet, the fountain which is the poet split open, and which sings for all.

The work of translation has taken me, then, from the piercing early lyrics through the poems of a first-rate poet at the height of his power, a world-poet raining music and experience upon all who will come to these poems.

He moved, says J. M. Cohen, in the same book, 'towards participation, but was driven back into solitude by lack of belief in his own existence,

> sobrecogio a mi espiritu una livida certidumbre:
> habia muerto el sol y una eterna noche amenecia.

Against this despair only one force could be set, the moment of experience outside time, which is the subject of Eliot's *Four Quartets....* Yet the experience itself never took clear shape; or rather many experiences masqueraded as the true one; vision and hallucination remained indistinguishable, and Freud, the Marquis de Sade, Rimbaud, André Breton and the Masters of Zen Buddhism were all accepted on a par as prophets of the new certainty that could be born out of utter negation.'

You have the poems here that mark the journey. 'The Prisoner' speaks for this place; 'Poetry'† describes the unreality, the situation itself. And here the poem is the hero, declaring and proving to the poet that he too exists, since the poem exists.

Paz has attempted, with his own voice, with the reach of his arms, to make the reconciliation among the opposites; where Aleixandre, who is seen by Cohen as parallel to Paz, moves 'in a direct line from solitude to participation, Paz, in three most important poems, sets out to reconcile the two opposites, solitude and utterance.' Two of the three poems are in this book: 'Himno entre ruinas' and 'Semillas para un himno'; the third,

* Included in *Configurations*, New Directions, N.Y., 1971.
† Not in present edition.

'Piedra de Sol,' is the last poem in *La estación violenta*, and Octavio Paz has chosen to include the entire rest of the book here.*

The movement onward in these poems was of great importance to me as translator, and *translator* is only a degree of *reader*. I broke during this part of the work, as the difficulties seemed beyond any chance of meeting. You will see innumerable places where the traces of my attempt to move from this poetry toward an English poem have left wounds, scars where we need healing. Sometimes I moved the names of trees; sometimes I made mistakes in my frenzy and ignorance, and was helped by others; sometimes a line like

> Una espiga es todo el trigo

refused to come over in any sound at all; sometimes I saw the lovers as giving kisses, when the Spanish *cambian* needed a term of trade. When you find these, and have better suggestions, give them to me. In the meantime, other poets have reached Paz. He is a world-poet, and he will come through in our lifetime, I think. There are fine translations by Denise Levertov, Paul Blackburn, Lysander Kemp, and there must be others that I have not heard. I hope eventually to make an edition in English, with the work of several hands, that will stand as a *Collected Poems*, or perhaps as *Collected Works*, as the essays, the play, and the translations from Basho appear.

The last book is an amazing achievement. Cohen writes, 'With the exception of T. S. Eliot, Octavio Paz is the only contemporary poet capable of feeling his metaphysics, and calling them to life.' From the concise poems in *Piedras Sueltas*—which I have translated as *Riprap*— to *The Violent Season*, the leap from the single image to the flow of the world can be felt.

A word about 'riprap.' I knew the word as a little girl whose father was engaged in the building of New York; I remember a time in class when I was asked what 'grit' was (I think the answer 'courage' may have been expected) and I answered 'Number Four gravel.' I had a paper returned for its too-esoteric fancy when I referred perfectly realistically to an orange-peel crane. But I bow here in the direction of Gary Snyder, who has called a book of his poems *Riprap*.

Octavio Paz has offered himself; this is what David Palmer is pre-figuring when he says, 'It is as if the author himself were a complex image.' There was this feeling during the reading given by Paz in New York, when his quiet, murderous, inflammatory, seductive voice struck home to an audience hearing these poems for the first time—in 1963. Then one could see what was happening.

* Note title changes and deletions in present edition.

As you can see it in this book, for his poems are here. The translator must be exposed to this extent; fully, that is. And the implications of the poems go deep, deep into the reader as witness, speaking for oneself as Paz speaks for himself, his land, his people. Carlos Fuentes, in a letter to me, says of 'El cantaro roto,' which burst upon Mexico in a wild stormy reception, 'I think that in this poem, Paz really creates the final, most lucid expression of Mexican tragedy: the country that dreams itself in the light, and lives itself in the dust and the thorns.'

The poetry of Octavio Paz is now recognized in the Hispanic world and is finding its poets and all its readers in other countries: France, Germany, Sweden, and now the United States. It has taken me a deep journey, and now its cycle finds again another beginning.

MURIEL RUKEYSER

ACKNOWLEDGMENT—1963 Edition

My thanks to Octavio Paz, for his many times of help and encouragement with the translation, and for the poems, which have meant very much reality to me in the reading and in the work with them; to Rizel Pincus, who went over my next-to-last drafts for correctness, with skill and poetry in her corrections (so that I often made many last drafts); to Elizabeth Hall, of the Bronx Botanical Gardens, for her help with *pirú;* to the Bollingen Foundation, for a translation grant to help with, in their phrase, 'two hundred lines'; and to Monica McCall, who with the affection of a friend and an agent, kept reminding me that the manuscript was due, due, and overdue.

Several passages from this translation were published in magazines including *Poetry, Chelsea Review, The Nation, Evergreen Review* and *Texas Quarterly*; in books, my *The Green Wave* and *Body of Waking* and Angel Flores' anthologies. Many of these poems have been read, by Octavio Paz, William Meredith, Paul Blackburn, myself, and others, at poetry centers, colleges, coffee houses, and broadcasts.

M. R.

PREFACE—1973 Edition

The growth of the work of Octavio Paz has made clear to an audience in many languages what was evident from the beginning, in these poems: he is a great poet, a world-poet whom we need. The poems here speak— as does all his work since—deeply, erotically, with grave and passionate involvement.

Since this first book of translations in English, many here have come to the poems of Paz as readers and many as translators. The *Foreword* above spoke of a hope that now is realized: in this book and in *Configurations* we have translations by several hands. Here is the reworking of the Paz into extraordinary poems in English by William Carlos Williams, Denise Levertov, Lysander Kemp, and Paul Blackburn. Other poets have also been translating Paz, and there will be books to come.

It has been a problem to move through the proprietary regulations of the Library of Congress regarding copyright, and the protective interests of publishers have worked both to guard and to exclude translators. I have removed my own translations to make way here, and I hope that we can go further in bringing the marvelous and necessary poems of Octavio Paz and other living poets to an English-speaking audience. The rules and functions now need to be looked at new. The fine poems can come through in fine variousness.

My thanks to Bernard Perry of the Indiana University Press for his long interest and the generosity which has allowed this transformation of *Selected Poems* into *Early Poems;* and to James Laughlin, who carried us through. Corrections of errors are, I hope, complete. Some new readings are in accordance with Octavio Paz's afterthoughts; to him, again and ever, thanks.

M. R.

New York, October, 1972

Contents

EARLY POEMS 1935-1955

Prólogo

Allá, donde terminan las fronteras, los caminos se borran. Donde se empieza el silencio. Avanzo lentamente y pueblo la noche de estrellas, de palabras, de la respiración de un agua remota que me espera donde comienza el alba.

Invento la víspera, la noche, el día siguiente que se levanta en su lecho de piedra y recorre con ojos límpidos un mundo penosamente soñado. Sostengo al árbol, a la nube, a la roca, al mar, presentimiento de dicha, invenciones que desfallecen y vacilan frente a la luz que disgrega.

Y luego la sierra árida, el caserío de adobe, la minuciosa realidad de un charco y un pirú estólido, de unos niños idiotas que me apedrean, de un pueblo rencoroso que me señala. Invento el terror, la esperanza, el mediodía—padre de los delirios solares, de las falacias espejeantes, de las mujeres que castran a sus amantes de una hora.

Invento la quemadura y el aullido, la masturbación en las letrinas, las visiones en el muladar, la prisión, el piojo y el chancro, la pelea por la sopa, la delación, los animales viscosos, los contactos innobles, los interrogatorios nocturnos, el examen de conciencia, el juez, la víctima, el testigo. Tú eres esos tres. ¿A quién apelar ahora y con qué argucias destruir al que te acusa? Inútiles los memoriales, los ayes y los alegatos. Inútil tocar a puertas condenadas. No hay puertas, hay espejos. Inútil cerrar los ojos o volver entre los hombres: esta lucidez ya no me abandona. Romperé los espejos, haré trizas mi imagen—que cada mañana rehace piadosamente mi cómplice, mi delator—. La soledad de la conciencia y la

Prologue

Out there, where the frontiers end, roads are erased. Where silence begins. I go forward slowly and I people the night with stars, with speech, with the breathing of distant water waiting for me where the dawn appears.

I invent evening, night, the next day rising from its bed of stone, the clear eyes of that day running across a world painfully dreamt. I sustain tree, cloud, rock, sea, the joy foreseen, inventions that vanish and hesitate before the light dispersed.

And then, the arid mountain, the adobe village, acute small reality of a puddle and one stolid peppertree, of some idiot children who stone me, a rancorous people which denounces me. I invent terror, hope, noon—father of solar frenzy, of glittering fallacies, of women who castrate their men of the hour.

I invent the burn and the howl, masturbation in latrines, visions in a dunghill, prison, lice, the chancre, the riot for soup, informers, viscous animals, low connections, interrogations at night, the inquiry into conscience, the judge, the victim, the witness. You are all three of them. To whom will you appeal now and with what sophistries will you annihilate the accuser? Petitions, appeals, allegations, all useless. Useless to knock on condemned doors. These are not doors, but mirrors. Useless to close one's eyes or to go back among men: this lucidity will never leave me. I will smash the mirrors, shatter my image to fragments—that each morning, mercifully, my accomplice, my accuser, recreates.—Solitude of

conciencia de la soledad, el día a pan y agua, la noche sin agua. Sequía, campo arrasado por un sol sin párpados, ojo atroz, oh conciencia, presente puro donde pasado y porvenir arden sin fulgor ni esperanza. Todo desemboca en esta eternidad que no desemboca.

Allá, donde los caminos se borran, donde acaba el silencio, invento la desesperación, la mente que me concibe, la mano que me dibuja, el ojo que me descubre. Invento al amigo que me inventa, mi semejante; y a la mujer, mi contrario: torre que corono de banderas, muralla que escalan mis espumas, ciudad devastada que renace lentamente bajo la dominación de mis ojos.

Contra el silencio y el bullicio invento la Palabra, libertad que se inventa y me inventa cada día.

consciousness and consciousness of solitude, day with its bread and water, night without water. Aridity, the country ravaged by a lidless sun, a frightful eye, oh consciousness, pure present where past and future burn with neither brilliance nor hope. Everything leads into this eternity which leads nowhere.

Out there, where the roads are erased, where silence ends, I invent despair, the mind that conceived me, the hand that designed me, the eye that discovered me. I invent the friend who invented me, my semblant; and woman, my contrary: tower crowned by me with banners, wall that my surf climbs, ruined city slowly reborn under the domination of my eyes.

Against silence and noise I invent the Word, freedom that invents itself and invents me every day.

El pájaro

Un silencio de aire, luz y cielo.
En el silencio transparente
el día reposaba:
la transparencia del espacio
era la transparencia del silencio.
La inmóvil luz del cielo sosegaba
el crecimiento de las yerbas.
Los bichos de la tierra, entre las piedras,
bajo una luz idéntica, eran piedras.
El tiempo en el minuto se saciaba.
En la quietud absorta
se consumaba el mediodía.

Y un pájaro cantó, delgada flecha.
Pecho de plata herido vibró el cielo,
se movieron las hojas,
las yerbas despertaron ...
Y sentí que la muerte era una flecha
que no se sabe quién dispara
y en un abrir los ojos nos morimos.

The bird

A silence of air, light, and sky.
In this transparent silence
day was resting:
the transparency of space
was silence's transparency.
Motionless light of the sky was soothing
the growth of the grass.
Small things of earth, among the stones,
under identical light, were stones.
Time sated itself in the minute.
And in an absorbed stillness
noonday consumed itself.

And a bird sang, slender arrow.
The sky shivered a wounded silver breast,
the leaves moved,
and grass awoke.
And I knew that death was an arrow
let fly from an unknown hand
and in the flicker of an eye we die.

Los novios

Tendidos en la yerba
una muchacha y un muchacho.
Comen naranjas, cambian besos
como las olas cambian sus espumas.

Tendidos en la playa
una muchacha y un muchacho.
Comen limones, cambian besos
como las nubes cambian sus espumas.

Tendidos bajo tierra
una muchacha y un muchacho.
No dicen nada, no se besan,
cambian silencio por silencio.

Engaged

Stretched out on the grass
a boy and a girl.
Sucking their oranges, giving their kisses
like waves exchanging foam.

Stretched out on the beach
a boy and a girl.
Sucking their limes, giving their kisses,
like clouds exchanging foam.

Stretched out underground
a boy and a girl.
Saying nothing, never kissing,
giving silence for silence.

Dos cuerpos

Dos cuerpos frente a frente
son a veces dos olas
y la noche es océano.

Dos cuerpos frente a frente
son a veces dos piedras
y la noche desierto.

Dos cuerpos frente a frente
son a veces raíces
en la noche enlazadas.

Dos cuerpos frente a frente
son a veces navajas
y la noche relámpago.

Dos cuerpos frente a frente
son dos astros que caen
en un cielo vacío.

Two bodies

Two bodies face to face
are at times two waves
and night is an ocean.

Two bodies face to face
are at times two stones
and night a desert.

Two bodies face to face
are at times two roots
laced into night.

Two bodies face to face
are at times two knives
and night strikes sparks.

Two bodies face to face
are two stars falling
in an empty sky.

Vida entrevista

Relámpagos o peces
en la noche del mar
y pájaros, relámpagos
en la noche del bosque.

Los huesos son relámpagos
en la noche del cuerpo.
Oh mundo, todo es noche
y la vida es relámpago.

Live interval

Lightning or fishes
in the night of the sea
and birds, lightning
in the forest night.

Our bones are lightning
in the night of the flesh.
O world, all is night,
life is the lightning.

Misterio

Relumbra el aire, relumbra,
el mediodía relumbra,
pero no veo al sol.

Y de presencia en presencia
todo se me transparenta,
pero no veo al sol.

Perdido en las transparencias
voy de reflejo a fulgor,
pero no veo al sol.

Y él en la luz se desnuda
y a cada esplendor pregunta,
pero no ve al sol.

Epitafio para un poeta

Quiso cantar, cantar
para olvidar
su vida verdadera de mentiras
y recordar
su mentirosa vida de verdades.

Mystery

Glittering of air, it glitters,
noon glitters here
but I see no sun

And from seeming to seeming
all is transparent,
but I see no sun.

Lost in transparencies
I move from reflection to blaze
but I see no sun.

The sun also is naked in the light
asking questions of every splendor,
but he sees no sun.

Poet's epitaph

He tried to sing, singing
not to remember
his true life of lies
and to remember
his lying life of truths.

Agua nocturna

La noche de ojos de caballo que tiemblan en la noche,
la noche de ojos de agua en el campo dormido,
está en tus ojos de caballo que tiembla,
está en tus ojos de agua secreta.

Ojos de agua de sombra,
ojos de agua de pozo,
ojos de agua de sueño.

El silencio y la soledad,
como dos pequeños animales a quienes guía la luna,
beben en esos ojos,
beben en esas aguas.

Si abres los ojos,
se abre la noche de puertas de musgo,
se abre el reino secreto del agua
que mana del centro de la noche.

Y si los cierras,
un ríote inuda por dentro,
avanza, te hare oscura:
la noche moja riberas en tu alma

Water night

Night with the eyes of a horse that trembles in the night,
night with eyes of water in the field asleep
is in your eyes, a horse that trembles,
is in your eyes of secret water.

Eyes of shadow-water,
eyes of well-water,
eyes of dream-water.

Silence and solitude,
two little animals moon-led,
drink in your eyes,
drink in those waters.

If you open your eyes,
night opens, doors of musk,
the secret kingdom of the water opens
flowing from the center of the night.

And if you close your eyes,
a river fills you from within,
flows forward, darkens you:
night brings its wetness to beaches in your soul.

Relámpago en reposo

Tendida,
piedra hecha de mediodía,
ojos entrecerrados donde el blanco azulea,
entornada sonrisa.
Te incorporas a medias y sacudes tu melena de león.
Luego te tiendes,
delgada estría de lava en la roca,
rayo dormido.
Mientras duermes te acaricio y te pulo,
hacha esbelta,
flecha con que incendio la noche.

El mar combate allá lejos con espadas y plumas.

Lightning at rest

Stretched out,
stone made of noon,
half-open eyes whose whiteness turns to blue,
half-ready smile.
Your body rouses, you shake your lion's mane.
Again lying down,
a fine striation of lava in the rock,
a sleeping ray of light.
And while you sleep I stroke you, I polish you,
slim axe,
arrow with whom I set the night on fire.

The sea fighting far off with its swords and feathers.

Más allá del amor

Todo nos amenaza:
el tiempo, que en vivientes fragmentos divide
al que fui
del que seré,
como el machete a la culebra;
la conciencia, la transparencia traspasada,
la mirada ciega de mirarse mirar;
las palabras, guantes grises, polvo mental sobre la yerba,
el agua, la piel;
nuestros nombres, que entre tú y yo se levantan,
murallas de vacío que ninguna trompeta derrumba.

Ni el sueño y su pueblo de imágenes rotas,
ni el delirio y su espuma profética,
ni el amor con sus dientes y uñas, nos bastan.
Más allá de nosotros,
en las fronteras del ser y el estar,
una vida más vida nos reclama.

Afuera la noche respira, se extiende,
llena de grandes hojas calientes,
de espejos que combaten:
frutos, garras, ojos, follajes,
espaldas que relucen,
cuerpos que se abren paso entre otros cuerpos.

Beyond love

Everything threatens us:
time, that in living fragments severs
what I have been
from what I will become,
as the machete splits the snake;
awareness, transparency pierced through,
the look blinded by seeing itself looking;
words, grey gloves, mental dust on the grass,
    water, skin;
our names, risen up between yourself and me,
walls of emptiness no trumpet can shout down.

Not dream, peopled with broken images,
nor delirium and its prophetic foam,
no, nor love with its teeth and claws, are enough.
Beyond ourselves,
on the frontier of being and becoming,
a life more alive claims us.

Outside, night breathes, and stretches,
full of its great warm leaves,
a war of mirrors:
fruit, talons, eyes, leafage,
backs that glisten,
bodies that make their way through other bodies.

Tiéndete aquí a la orilla de tanta espuma,
de tanta vida que se ignora y entrega:
tú también perteneces a la noche.
Extiéndete, blancura que respira,
late, estrella repartida,
copa,
pan que inclinas la balanza del lado de la aurora,
pausa de sangre entre este tiempo y otro sin medida.

Lie here stretched out on the shore of so much foam,
of so much life unconscious and surrendered:
you too belong to the night.
Lie down, stretch out, you are whiteness and breathing,
throb, star divided,
drink and glass,
bread that weighs down the scales on the side of daybreak,
pause of the blood between now and measureless time.

El día abre la mano
Tres nubes
Y estas pocas palabras

Al alba busca su nombre lo naciente
Sobre los troncos soñolientos centellea la luz
Galopan las montañas a la orilla del mar
El sol entra en las aguas con espuelas
La piedra embiste y rompe claridades
El mar se obstina y crece al pie del horizonte
Tierra confusa inminencia de escultura
El mundo alza la frente aún desnuda
Piedra pulida y lisa para grabar un canto
La luz despliega su abanico de nombres
Hay un comienzo de himno como un árbol
Hay el viento y nombres hermosos en el viento

(Untitled)

The hand of day opens
Three clouds
And these few words

(Untitled)

At daybreak the newborn goes looking for a name
Upon the sleep-filled bodies the light glitters
The mountains gallop to the shore of the sea
The sun with his spurs on is entering the waves
Stony attack shattering clarities
The sea resists rearing to the horizon
Confusion of land imminence of sculpture
The naked forehead of the world is raised
Rock smoothed and polished to cut a poem on
Display of light that opens its fan of names
Here is the seed of a singing like a tree
Here are the wind and names beautiful in the wind

Fábula

Edades de fuego y de aire
Mocedades de agua
Del verde al amarillo
   Del amarillo al rojo
Del sueño a la vigilia
   Del deseo al acto
Sólo había un paso que tú dabas sin esfuerzo
Los insectos eran joyas animadas
El calor reposaba al borde del estanque
La lluvia era un sauce de pelo suelto
En la palma de tu mano crecía un árbol
Aquel árbol cantaba reía y profetizaba
Sus vaticinios cubrían de alas el espacio
Había milagros sencillos llamados pájaros
Todo era de todos
   Todos eran todo
Sólo había una palabra inmensa y sin revés
Palabra como un sol
Un día se rompió en fragmentos diminutos
Son las palabras del lenguaje que hablamos
Fragmentos que nunca se unirán
Espejos rotos donde el mundo se mira destrozado

Fable

The age of fire and the age of air
The youth of water springing
From green to yellow
                    Yellow to red
From dream to vigil
                    From desire to act
You needed only a step and that taken without effort
The insects then were jewels who were alive
The heat lay down to rest at the edge of the pool
Rain was the light hair of a willow-tree
There was a tree growing within your hand
And as it grew it sang laughed prophesied
It cast the spells that cover space with wings
There were the simple miracles called birds
Everything belonged to everyone
                    Everyone was everything
Only one word existed immense without opposite
A word like a sun
One day exploded into smallest fragments
They were the words of the language that we speak
They are the splintered mirrors where the world
                    can see itself   slaughtered

Una mujer de movimientos de río
De transparentes ademanes de agua
Una muchacha de agua
Donde leer lo que pasa y no regresa
Un poco de agua donde los ojos beban
Donde los labios de un solo sorbo beban
El árbol la nube el relámpago
Yo mismo y la muchacha

(Untitled)

A woman whose movements are a river's
Transparent gesturing that water has
A girl made of water
Where may be read the irreversible present
A little water where the eyes may drink
The lips swallow in a long single drink
The tree the cloud the lamp
Myself and that girl

A la española el día entra pisando fuerte
Un rumor de hojas y pájaros avanza
Un presentimiento de mar o mujeres
El día zumba en mi frente como una idea fija
En la frente del mundo zumba tenaz el día
La luz corre por todas partes
Canta por las terrazas
Hace bailar las casas
Bajo las manos frescas de la yedra ligera
El muro se despierta y levanta sus torres
Y las piedras dejan caer sus vestiduras
Y el agua se desnuda y salta de su lecho
Más desnuda que el agua
Y la luz se desnuda y se mira en el agua
Más desnuda que un astro
Y el pan se abre y el vino se derrama
Y el día se derrama sobre el agua tendida
Ver oír tocar oler gustar pensar
Labios o tierra o viento entre veleros
Sabor del día que se desliza como música
Rumor de luz que lleva de la mano a una muchacha
Y la deja desnuda en el centro del día
Nadie sabe su nombre ni a qué vino
Como un poco de agua se tiende a mi costado
El sol se para un instante por mirarla
La luz se pierde entre sus piernas
La rodean mis miradas como agua
Y ella se baña en ellas más desnuda que el agua
Como la luz no tiene nombre propio
Como la luz cambia de forma con el día

(Untitled)

Day enters stamping like a Spanish dancer
A rumor of leaves and birds flies forward
Presentiment of women or of waves
Day buzzes in my head like an obsession
In the head of the world it buzzes obstinate day
Light races everywhere
Sings on the hillsides
Makes houses dance
Under the cool hands of the light ivy
The wall awakens and lifts up its towers
And the rocks let their clothes slip down
And water is laid bare and naked leaps
More naked from its bed than water is
And light is naked and sees itself in water
More naked than a star
And bread is broken and wine is poured
And day is poured over the outspread water
To see hear touch smell taste think
Lips or land or breeze between sailboats
Taste of day that moves along like music
Rumor of light that leads a girl by the hand
Leaving her naked at the core of day
Nobody knows her name or why she has come here
Like so much water she stretches out beside me
The sun stands still for a moment to stare at her
And light loses itself between her legs
As by water she is surrounded by my gaze
And in them bathes more naked than the water
Like light she has no name that is her own
Like light she changes form as the day changes

Día

Un día se pierde
En el cielo hecho de prisa
La luz no deja huellas en la nieve
Un día se pierde
Abrir y cerrar de puertas
La semilla del sol se abre sin ruido
Un día comienza
La niebla asciende la colina
Un hombre baja por el río
Los dos se encuentran en tus ojos
Y tú te pierdes en el día
Cantando en el follaje de la luz
Tañen campanas allá lejos
Cada llamada es una ola
Cada ola sepulta para siempre
Un gesto una palabra la luz contra la nube
Tú ríes y te peinas distraída
Un día comienza a tus pies
Pelo mano blancura no son nombres
Para este pelo esta mano esta blancura
Lo visible y palpable que está afuera
Lo que está adentro y sin nombre
A tientas se buscan en nosotros
Siguen la marcha del lenguaje
Cruzan el puente que les tiende esta imagen
Como la luz entre los dedos se deslizan
Como tú misma entre mis manos
Como tu mano entre mis manos se entrelazan
Un día comienza en mis palabras
Luz que madura hasta ser cuerpo
Hasta ser sombra de tu cuerpo luz de tu sombra
Malla de calor piel de tu luz
Un día comienza en tu boca
El día que se abre en nuestra noche

Day

A day is lost
In a sky suddenly there
Light leaves no footprints in the snow
A day is lost
Opening and shutting of doors
The seed of the sun splits open soundlessly
A day begins
The fog goes up in the foothills
A man goes down to the river
They meet and are found in your eyes
And you lose yourself in day
Singing among the leaves of light
Sounds of bells far away
Every call a wave
Every wave obliterates
A gesture, a word, the light against cloud
You laugh and you do your hair not noticing
A day begins at your feet
Skin hand whiteness these are not names
For this skin this hand and this whiteness
The visible and palpable which is outside
That which is within and is nameless
By acts of touch they go searching in us
Following the turns that language made
Crossing the bridge this image strung from them
As light pouring itself among the fingers
As you yourself between my hands
As your hand interlaced within my hands
A day begins in my words
Light which goes ripening until it becomes flesh
Until it becomes shadow of your flesh light of your shadow
Network of warmth skin of your light
A day begins in your mouth
Day which opens in our night

Piedra nativa

La luz devasta las alturas
Manadas de imperios en derrota
El ojo retrocede cercado de reflejos

Países vastos como el insomnio
Pedregales de hueso

Otoño sin confines
Alza la sed sus invisibles surtidores
Un último pirú predica en el desierto

Cierra los ojos y oye cantar la luz:
El mediodía anida en tu tímpano

Cierra los ojos y ábrelos:
No hay nadie ni siquiera tú mismo
Lo que no es piedra es luz

Native stone

Light is laying waste the heavens
Droves of dominions in stampede
The eye retreats surrounded by mirrors

Landscapes enormous as insomnia
Stony ground of bone

Limitless autumn
Thirst lifts its invisible fountains
One last peppertree preaches in the desert

Close your eyes and hear the song of the light:
Noon takes shelter in your inner ear

Close your eyes and open them:
There is nobody not even yourself
Whatever is not stone is light

Refranes

Una espiga es todo el trigo
Una pluma un pájaro vivo y cantando
Un hombre de carne es un hombre de sueño
La verdad no se parte
El trueno proclama los hechos del relámpago
Una mujer soñada encarna siempre en una forma amada
El árbol dormido pronuncia verdes oráculos
El agua habla sin cesar y nunca se repite
En la balanza de unos párpados el sueño no pesa
En la balanza de una lengua que delira
Una lengua de mujer que dice sí a la vida
El ave del paraíso abre las alas

Como la marejada verde de marzo en el campo
Entre los años de sequía te abres paso
Nuestras miradas se cruzan se entrelazan
Tejen un transparente vestido de fuego
Una yedra dorada que te cubre
Alta y desnuda sonríes como la catedral el día del incendio
Con el mismo gesto de la lluvia en el trópico lo has
    arrasado todo
Los días harapientos caen a nuestros pies
No hay nada sino dos seres desnudos y abrazados
Un surtidor en el centro de la pieza
Manantiales que duermen con los ojos abiertos
Jardines de agua flores de agua piedras preciosas de agua
Verdes monarquías

La noche de jade gira lentamente sobre sí misma

Proverbs

One sheaf of wheat is the whole wheat field
One feather is a bird alive and singing
A man of flesh is a man of dream
Truth is indivisible
One clap of thunder proclaims the acts of the lightning
One dreaming woman gives us the form of love forever
The sleeping tree speaks all green oracles
Water talks ceaseless never repeating a word
Judged against certain eyelids, sleep is nothing
Judged by a mouth, a tongue that is crying out
The tongue of a woman saying Yes to life
The bird of paradise opening his wings

(Untitled)

Like the green surf of April in the fields
Between the years of drought you open a way
Now the looks of our eyes are met are laced together
They weave a transparent cloth out of this fire
Ivy of gold to cover you
Tall and naked you smile the cathedral the day of the fire
With the same gesture the rain makes in the tropics washing
    all away
The days in their rags fall down at our feet
There is nothing in the world but two beings naked embraced
A fountain in the middle of the room
Springs of origin sleeping with open eyes
Gardens of water flowers of water precious stones of water
Green sovereignties

The night of jade turns slowly upon itself

Semillas para un himno

Infrecuentes (pero también inmerecidas)
Instantáneas (pero es verdad que el tiempo no se mide
Hay instantes que estallan y son astros
Otros son un río detenido y unos árboles fijos
Otros son ese mismo río arrasando los mismos árboles)
Infrecuentes
          Instantáneas noticias favorables
Dos o tres nubes de cristal de roca
Horas altas como la marea
Estrépito de plumas blancas en el cielo nocturno
Islas en llamas en mitad del Pacífico
Mundos de imágenes suspendidos de un hilo de araña
Y entre todos la muchacha que avanza partiendo en dos las
    altas aguas
Como el sol la muchacha que se abre paso como la llama
    que avanza
Como el viento partiendo en dos la cortina de nubes
Velero
Relámpago partiendo en dos al tiempo
Tus hombros tienen la marca de los dientes del amor
La noche polar arde
Infrecuentes
          Instantáneas noticias del mundo
(Cuando el mundo entreabre sus puertas y el ángel cabecea a la
    entrada del jardín)
Nunca merecidas
          (Todo se nos da por añadidura
En una tierra condenada a repetirse sin tregua
Todos somos indignos

Seeds for a psalm

Seldom (but nevertheless undeserved)
Sudden (but certainly time is measureless
There are moments that explode and become stars
Some are a river in check and a few unmoving trees
Some are that same river uprooting those same trees)
Seldom
       Sudden good news
Two or three clouds of rock-crystal
Hours tall as high tide
Crash of white plumes in the night sky
Islands in flames in mid-Pacific
Worlds made of images suspended from spiderweb
And among them all the girl who comes forward dividing the
    deep waters
Like the sun the girl who rushes like
    flame advancing
Like the wind dividing the curtain of clouds
Sailboat
Lightning-flash dividing time
Your shoulders carry the mark of the teeth of love
The polar night on fire
Seldom
       Sudden news of the world
(When the world begins to open its doors and the angel nods
    consent at the gate of the garden)
Never deserved
        (Everything is given to us, on top of everything
In a land condemned to repeat itself without respite
We are all unworthy

Hasta los muertos enrojecen
Hasta los ciegos deletrean la escritura del látigo
Racimos de mendigos cuelgan de las ciudades
Casas de ira torres de frente obtusa)
Infrecuentes
                    Instantáneas
No llegan siempre en forma de palabras
Brota una espiga de unos labios
Una forma veloz abre las alas
                              Imprevistas
Instantáneas
Como en la infancia cuando decíamos "ahí viene un barco
    cargado de ..."
Y brotaba instantánea imprevista la palabra convocada
            Pez
                Alamo
                    Colibrí
Y así ahora de mi frente zarpa un barco cargado de iniciales
Ávidas de encarnar en imágenes
                              Instantáneas
Imprevistas cifras del mundo
La luz se abre en las terrazas del mediodía
Se interna en el bosque como una sonámbula
Penetra en el cuerpo dormido del agua

Por un instante están los nombres habitados

Even the dead blush
Even the blind decipher the whip's writing
Clusters of beggars are hanging from the cities
Houses of wrath towers with dull faces)
Seldom
      Sudden
They do not always arrive in the form of words
A spike of grain bursts from some lips
A swift form opens its wings
                    Unforeseen
Sudden
As in early childhood when we said "here comes a ship with a
    load of ..."
And suddenly unforeseen the word evoked burst forth
      Fish
          Willow
              Humming-bird
And so now from my head sails a ship with a load of initials
Avid for incarnation in images
                    Sudden
Unforeseen ciphers of the world
Light opens on the terraces of noon
Enters the forest like a sleepwalker
Penetrates the sleeping body of the water

For a moment life quickens in the names

Lección de cosas

1. ANIMACION

Sobre el librero,
entre un músico Tang y un jarro de Oaxaca,
incandescente y vivaz,
con chispeantes ojos de papel de plata,
nos mira ir y venir
la pequeña calavera de azúcar.

2. MASCARA DE TLALOC GRABADA EN CUARZO TRANSPARENTE

Aguas petrificadas.
El viejo Tláloc duerme, dentro,
soñando temporales.

3. LO MISMO

Tocado por la luz
el cuarzo ya es cascada.
Sobre sus aguas flota, niño, el dios.

4. DIOS QUE SURGE DE UNA ORQUIDEA DE BARRO

Entre los pétalos de arcilla
nace, sonriente,
la flor humana.

Object lesson

1. ANIMATION

Over the bookcase
between a Tang musician and an Oaxaca pitcher
incandescent, lively,
with glittering eyes of silver-paper
watching us come and go
the little sugar skull.

2. MASK OF TLALOC CARVED IN TRANSPARENT QUARTZ

Petrified waters.
Old Tlaloc sleeps, within,
dreaming rainstorms.

3. THE SAME

Touched by light
quartz has become cascade.
Upon its waters floats the child, the god.

4. GOD WHO COMES FORTH FROM A CERAMIC ORCHID

Among clay petals
is born, smiling,
the human flower.

5. DIOSA OLMECA

Los cuatro puntos cardinales
regresan a tu ombligo.
En tu vientre golpea el día, armado.

6. CALENDARIO

Contra el agua, días de fuego.
Contra el fuego, días de agua.

7. XOCHIPILLI

En el árbol del día
cuelgan frutos de jade,
fuego y sangre en la noche.

8. CRUZ CON SOL Y LUNA PINTADOS

Entre los brazos de esta cruz
anidaron dos pájaros:
Adán, sol, y Eva, luna.

9. NIÑO Y TROMPO

Cada vez que lo lanza,
cae, justo,
en el centro del mundo.

10. OBJETOS

Viven a nuestro lado,
los ignoramos, nos ignoran.
Alguna vez conversan con nosotros.

5. OLMEC GODDESS

The four cardinal points
are gathered in your navel.
In your womb the day is pounding, fully armed.

6. CALENDAR

Facing water, days of fire.
Facing fire, days of water.

7. XOCHIPILLI

In a day's tree
hang jade fruit,
fire and blood at night

8. CROSS WITH SUN AND MOON PAINTED ON IT

Between the arms of this cross
two birds made their nest:
Adam, sun, and Eve, moon.

9. BOY AND TOP

Each time he spins it,
it lands, precisely,
at the center of the world.

10. OBJECTS

They live alongside us,
we do not know them, they do not know us.
But sometimes they speak with us.

En Uxmal

1. TEMPLO DE LAS TORTUGAS

En la explanada vasta como el sol
reposa y danza el sol de piedra,
desnudo frente al sol, también desnudo.

2. MEDIODIA

La luz no parpadea,
el tiempo se vacía de minutos,
se ha detenido un pájaro en el aire.

3. MAS TARDE

Se despeña la luz,
despiertan las columnas
y, sin moverse, bailan.

4. PLENO SOL

La hora es transparente:
vemos, si es invisible el pájaro,
el color de su canto.

5. RELIEVES

La lluvia, pie danzante y largo pelo,
el tobillo mordido por el rayo,
desciende acompañada de tambores:
abre los ojos el maíz, y crece.

46

In Uxmal

In this court vast as the sun
rests and dances a stone sun,
naked before the sun; he too is naked.

2. NOON

Light unblinking,
time empty of minutes,
a bird stopped short in air.

3. LATER

Light flung down,
the pillars awake
and, without moving, dance.

4. FULL SUN

The time is transparent:
even if the bird is invisible,
let us see the color of his song.

5. RELIEFS

The rain, dancing, long-haired,
ankles slivered by lightning,
descends, to an accompaniment of drums:
the corn opens its eyes, and grows.

6. SERPIENTE LABRADA SOBRE UN MURO

El muro al sol respira, vibra, ondula,
trozo de cielo vivo y tatuado:
el hombre bebe sol, es agua, es tierra.
Y sobre tanta vida la serpiente
que lleva una cabeza entre las fauces:
los dioses beben sangre, comen hombres.

6. SERPENT CARVED ON A WALL

The wall in the sun breathes, shivers, ripples,
a live and tattooed fragment of the sky:
a man drinks sun and is water, is earth.
And over all that life the serpent
carrying a head between his jaws:
the gods drink blood, the gods eat man.

Piedras sueltas

1. FLOR

El grito, el pico, el diente, los aullidos,
la nada carnicera y su barullo,
ante esta simple flor se desvanecen.

2. DAMA

Todas las noches baja al pozo
y a la mañana reaparece
con un nuevo reptil entre los brazos.

3. BIOGRAFIA

No lo que pudo ser:
es lo que fue.
Y lo que fue está muerto.

4. CAMPANAS EN LA NOCHE

Olas de sombra, olas de ceguera
sobre una frente en llamas:
mojad mi pensamiento, ¡y apagadlo!

5. ANTE LA PUERTA

Gentes, palabras, gentes.
Dudé un instante:
la luna arriba, sola.

Riprap

1. FLOWER

Cry, barb, tooth, howls,
carnivorous nothingness, its turbulence,
all disappear before this simple flower.

2. SHE

Every night she goes down to the well
next morning reappearing
with a new reptile in her arms.

3. BIOGRAPHY

Not what he might have been:
but what he was.
And what he was is dead.

4. BELLS IN THE NIGHT

Waves of shadows, waves of blindness
on a forehead in flames:
water for my thought, drown it out!

5. AT THE DOOR

People, words, people.
I hesitated:
up there the moon, alone.

6. VISION

Me vi al cerrar los ojos:
espacio, espacio
donde estoy y no estoy.

7. PAISAJE

Los insectos atareados,
los caballos color de sol,
los burros color de nube,
las nubes, rocas enormes que no pesan,
los montes como cielos desplomados,
la manada de árboles bebiendo en el arroyo,
todos están ahí, dichosos en su estar,
frente a nosotros que no estamos,
comidos por la rabia, por el odio,
por el amor comidos, por la muerte.

6. VISION

I saw myself when I shut my eyes:
space, space
where I am and am not.

7. LANDSCAPE

Insects endlessly busy,
horses the color of sun,
donkeys the color of cloud,
clouds, huge rocks that weigh nothing,
mountains like tilted skies,
a flock of trees drinking at the stream,
they are all there, delighted in being there,
and here we are not who are not,
eaten by fury, by hatred,
by love eaten, by death.

Ni el cielo ni la tierra

Atrás el cielo,
atrás la luz y su navaja,
atrás los muros de salitre,
atrás las calles que dan siempre a otras calles.

Atrás mi piel de vidrios erizados,
atrás mis uñas y mis dientes
caídos en el pozo del espejo.
Atrás la puerta que se cierra,
el cuerpo que se abre.
Atrás, amor encarnizado,
pureza que destruye,
garras de seda, labios de ceniza.

Atrás, tierra o cielo.

Sentados a las mesas
donde beben la sangre de los pobres:
la mesa del dinero,
la mesa de la gloria y la de la justicia,
la mesa del poder y la mesa de Dios
—la Sagrada Familia en su Pesebre,
la Fuente de la Vida,
el espejo quebrado en que Narciso
a sí mismo se bebe y no se sacia
y el hígado, alimento de profetas ye buitres ...

Atrás, tierra o cielo.

Nor heaven nor earth

Away with heaven,
away with the light and its razor,
away with saltpeter walls,
away with streets that open forever on more streets.

Away with the bristling windows of my skin,
away with my nails and my teeth
fallen into the well of the mirror.
Away with the door that is shut,
the body that opens.
Away with carnivorous love,
destructive purity,
silk claws, lips of ashes.

Away with earth or heaven.

Seated at the tables
where they drink the blood of the poor:
the table of money,
the tables of glory and of justice,
the table of power and the table of God
—the Holy Family in its Manger,
the Fountain of Life,
the broken mirror where Narcissus
drinks of himself and does not slake his thirst
and the liver, food of prophets and vultures ...

Away with earth or heaven.

Cohabitando escondidos
en sábanas insomnes,
cuerpos de cal y yeso,
piedras, cenizas ateridas
cuando la luz los toca;
y las tumbas de piedras o palabras,
la torre de Babel en comandita
y el cielo que bosteza
y el infierno mordiéndose la cola
y la resurrección
y el día de la vida perdurable,
el día sin crepúsculo,
el paraíso visceral del feto.

Creía en todo esto.
Hoy canto solo
a la orilla del llanto.
También el llanto sirve de almohada.

Cohabiting secretly
on sleepless sheets,
bodies of lime and plaster,
stones, ashes stiff with cold
when the light touches them;
and tombs built of stones or words,
their silent partner, the tower of Babel
and the yawning sky
and hell biting its own tail
and the resurrection
and the day of life that persists and endures,
day without twilight,
the visceral paradise of the embryo.

I used to believe in all this.
Today I sing alone
on a shore of wailing.
Wailing, too, will do for a pillow.

Las palabras

Dales la vuelta,
cógelas del rabo (chillen, putas),
azótalas,
dales azúcar en la boca a las rejegas,
ínflalas, globos, pínchalas,
sórbeles sangre y tuétanos,
sécalas,
cápalas,
písalas, gallo galante,
tuérceles el gaznate, cocinero,
desplúmalas,
destrípalas, toro,
buey, arrástralas,
hazlas, poeta,
has que se traguen todas sus palabras.

Words

Go at it again,
fling them around,
give it to them,
let them bitch, the whores,
whip them,
put sugar in their mouths,
blow them up, globes, pinch them,
suck their blood and marrow,
dry them up,
cut their balls,
cover them, cock of the walk,
wring their necks, cook,
pluck them,
rip their guts out, bull,
drag them down, bullock,
make them, poet,
make them eat their own words.

Escritura

Cuando sobre el papel la pluma escribe,
a cualquier hora solitaria,
¿quién la guía?
¿A quién escribe el que escribe por mí,
orilla hecha de labios y de sueño,
quieta colina, golfo,
hombro para olvidar al mundo para siempre?

Alguien escribe en mí, mueve mi mano,
escoge una palabra, se detiene,
duda entre el mar azul y el monte verde.
Con un ardor helado
contempla lo que escribo.
Todo lo quema, fuego justiciero.
Pero este juez también es víctima
y al condenarme, se condena:
no escribe a nadie, a nadie llama,
a sí mismo se escribe, en sí se olvida,
y se rescata, y vuelve a ser yo mismo.

Writing

When over the paper the pen goes writing
in any solitary hour,
who drives the pen?
To whom is he writing, he who writes for me,
this shore made of lips, made of dream,
a hill of stillness, abyss,
shoulder on which to forget the world forever?

Someone in me is writing, moves my hand,
hears a word, hesitates,
halted between green mountain and blue sea.
With icy fervor
contemplates what I write.
All is burned in this fire of justice.
But this judge is nevertheless the victim
and in condemning me condemns himself:
He writes to anyone, he calls nobody,
to his own self he writes, and in himself forgets,
and is redeemed, becoming again me.

Razones para morir

I

Unos me hablaban de la patria.
Mas yo pensaba en una tierra pobre,
pueblo de polvo y luz,
y una calle y un muro
y un hombre silencioso junto al muro.
Y aquellas piedras bajo el sol del páramo
y la luz que en el río se desnuda ...
olvidos que alimentan la memoria,
que ni nos pertenecen ni llamamos,
sueños del sueño, súbitas presencias
con las que el tiempo dice que no somos,
que es él quien se recuerda y él quien sueña.
No hay patria, hay tierra, imágenes de tierra,
polvo y luz en el tiempo ...

2

La rima que se acuesta con todas las palabras,
la Libertad, a muerte me llamaba,
alcahueta, sirena
de garganta leprosa.
Virgen de humo de mi adolescencia
mi libertad me sonreía
como un abismo contemplado
desde el abismo de nosotros mismos.

Reasons for dying

1

Some spoke of our land.
But I thought of a poor earth,
people of dust and light,
a street and a wall
and a silent man up against the wall.
And those stones in the clear upland sun
and light standing naked in the river ...
forgotten things that feed my memory,
irrelevant things, not summoned up,
dreams of a dream, those sudden presences
with which time tells us that we have no being,
that time is the one who remembers and who dreams.
There is no country, there is earth and its images,
dust and light living in time ...

2

The rhyme which goes to bed with all the words,
Freedom, has been calling me to death,
she runs the whorehouse, siren
whose throat is leprosy.
Smoky virgin of my adolescence
my freedom used to smile at me
like an abyss observed
from that abyss, our selves.

La libertad es alas,
es el viento entre hojas, detenido
por una simple flor; y el sueño
en el que somos nuestro sueño;
es morder la naranja prohibida,
abrir la vieja puerta condenada
y desatar al prisionero:
esa piedra ya es pan,
esos papeles blancos son gaviotas,
son pájaros las hojas
y pájaros tus dedos: todo vuela.

Freedom is wings,
the wind in leaves, pausing over
a simple flower: and the sleep
in which we are our dream;
it is the eating of forbidden fruit,
the opening of the old abandoned gate
untying the prisoner:
that stone is bread,
those white papers are seagulls,
the leaves are birds,
your fingers birds: everything is in flight.

Seven p.m.

En filas ordenadas regresamos
y cada noche, cada noche,
mientras hacemos el camino,
el breve infierno de la espera
y el espectro que vierte en el oído:
"¿No tienes sangre ya? ¿Por qué te mientes?
Mira los pájaros ...
El mundo tiene playas todavía
y un barco allá te espera, siempre."

Y las piernas caminan
y una roja marea
inunda playas de ceniza.

"Es hermosa la sangre
cuando salta de ciertos cuellos blancos.
Báñate en esa sangre:
el crimen hace dioses."

Y el hombre aprieta el paso
y ve la hora: aún es tiempo
de alcanzar el tranvía.

"Allá, del otro lado,
yacen las islas prometidas. Danzan
los árboles de música vestidos,
se mecen las naranjas en las ramas
y las granadas abren sus entrañas
y se desgranan en la yerba,
rojas estrellas en un cielo verde,
para la aurora de amarilla cresta ..."

Seven p.m.

We go back in orderly rows
and every night, every night,
while we go that journey,
the little hell of hope
and the ghost who spills in your ears:
"No blood in your veins? Why lie?
Look, the birds ...
The world is there with its beaches
and far out there's a ship waiting for you, forever."

And legs walk
and red surf
floods beaches of ashes.

"Lovely, that blood
as it leaps from certain white throats.
Bathe in that blood:
crime makes gods."

And the man quickens his step,
he knows what time it is: now it is time
to catch the streetcar.

"Far out, on the other shore,
lie the promised isles. Trees
robed in music dance their dance,
oranges swing on those branches,
pomegranates split open
and spill their seeds on the grass,
red stars on a sky of green,
in yellow-crested dawn ..."

Y los labios sonríen y saludan
a otros condenados solitarios:
¿Leyó usted los periódicos?

"¿No dijo que era el Pan y que era el Vino?
¿No dijo que era al Agua?
Cuerpos dorados como el pan dorado
y el vino de labios morados
y el agua, desnudez ..."

Y el hombre aprieta el paso
y al tiempo justo de llegar a tiempo
doblan la esquina, puntuales, Dios y el tranvía.

And lips smile and greet
others in solitary:
Have you seen the papers?

"Didn't he say I was the Bread and the Wine?
Didn't he say I was the Water?
Bodies made gold like bread made gold
and wine of purple lips
and water, nakedness ..."

And the man quickens his step
and at exactly the time of being on time
they turn the corner, punctual, God and the streetcar.

La calle

Es una calle larga y silenciosa.
Ando en tinieblas y tropiezo y caigo
y me levanto y piso con pies ciegos
las piedras mudas y las hojas secas
y alguien detrás de mí también las pisa:
si me detengo, se detiene;
si corro, corre. Vuelvo el rostro: nadie.
Todo está oscuro y sin salida,
y doy vueltas y vueltas en esquinas
que dan siempre a la calle
donde nadie me espera ni me sigue,
donde yo sigo a un hombre que tropieza
y se levanta y dice al verme: nadie.

The street

A long and silent street.
I walk in blackness and I stumble and fall
and rise, and I walk blind, my feet
stepping on silent stones and dry leaves.
Someone behind me also stepping on stones, leaves:
if I slow down, he slows;
if I run, he runs. I turn: nobody.
Everything dark and doorless.
Turning and turning among these corners
which lead forever to the street
where nobody waits for, nobody follows me,
where I pursue a man who stumbles
and rises and says when he sees me: nobody.

Elegía interrumpida

Hoy recuerdo a los muertos de mi casa.
Al primer muerto nunca lo olvidamos,
aunque muera de rayo, tan aprisa
que no alcance la cama ni los óleos.
Oigo el bastón que duda en un peldaño,
el cuerpo que se afianza en un suspiro,
la puerta que se abre, el muerto que entra.
De una puerta a morir hay poco espacio
y apenas queda tiempo de sentarse,
alzar la cara, ver la hora
y enterarse: las ocho y cuarto.
Y oigo el reloj que da la hora,
terco reloj que marca siempre el paso,
y nunca avanza y nunca retrocede.

Hoy recuerdo a los muertos de mi casa.
La que murió noche tras noche
y era una larga despedida,
un tren que nunca parte, su agonía.
Codicia de la boca
al hilo de un suspiro suspendida,
ojos que no se cierran y hacen señas
y vagan de la lámpara a mis ojos,
fija mirada que se abraza a otra,
ajena, que se asfixia en el abrazo
y al fin se escapa y ve desde la orilla
cómo se hunde y pierde cuerpo el alma
y no encuentra unos ojos a que asirse ...
¿Y me invitó a morir esa mirada?

Interrupted elegy

Now I remember the dead of my own house.
We never forget the first among us dead,
though he was the one struck down, he died so fast
that nothing was there, no bed, no holy oils.
I hear the cane falter on a step of the stairs,
the body that makes itself secure, sighing,
the door opening, the dead man coming in.
Between a door and dying there's little space,
and there's hardly time enough to settle in,
look up and see what time it is
and find out: it's exactly quarter past eight.
And I hear the clock that says what time it is,
obstinate clock that is always marking time,
and never gains and never falls behind.

Now I remember the dead of my own house.
The woman, the one who died night after night
and that was certainly a long leave-taking,
a train that never started, her agony.
Covetousness of the mouth
suspended on the thread of a sighing breath,
eyes that never close, eyes that send out signals
and wander from the lamp to my own eyes,
rigid stare which embraces another look,
the distant one, suffocating in embrace
and finally escapes and watches from the shore
how the soul is submerged and loses body
and never finds eyes that it can fasten on ...
And was it this stare that summoned me to death?

Quizá morir con otro no es morirse.
Quizá morimos sólo porque nadie
quiere morirse con nosotros, nadie
quiere mirarnos a los ojos.

Hoy recuerdo a los muertos de mi casa.
Al que se fue por unas horas
y nadie sabe dónde se ha perdido
ni a qué silencio entró.
De sobremesa, cada noche,
la pausa sin color que da al vacío
o la frase sin fin que cuelga a medias
del hilo de la araña del silencio
abren un corredor para el que vuelve:
suenan sus pasos, sube, se detiene ...
Y alguien entre nosotros se levanta
y cierra bien la puerta.
Pero él, allá del otro lado, insiste.
Acecha en cada hueco, en los repliegues,
vaga entre los bostezos, las afueras.
No se ha muerto del todo, se ha perdido.
Y aunque cerremos puertas, él insiste.

Hoy recuerdo a los muertos de mi casa.
Rostros perdidos en mi frente, rostros
sin ojos, ojos fijos, vaciados,
¿busco en ellos acaso mi secreto,
el dios de sangre que mi sangre mueve,
el dios de hielo, el dios que me devora?
Su silencio es espejo de mi vida,
en mi vida su muerte se prolonga:
soy el error final de sus errores.

Hoy recuerdo a los muertos de mi casa.
El círculo falaz del pensamiento
que desemboca siempre donde empieza,
la saliva que es polvo, que es ceniza,
los labios mentirosos, la mentira,

Perhaps to die with someone is not to die.
Perhaps we die only because nobody
is willing to die with us, nobody
is willing to look us in the eyes.

Now I remember the dead of my own house.
He who was absent for a matter of hours
and nobody knows the place where he is lost
nor what silence he has entered.
After dinner, every evening,
the colorless pause which leads to emptiness
or the endless sentence which is partly hanging
upon the shining spiderweb of silence
open a corridor for one returning:
we hear his footsteps, he climbs the stair, he stops ...
And someone or other among us gets up
and shuts the door tight.
But he, out there on the other side, insists.
He lies in ambush in every hole and fold,
he is wandering among the yawns, the suburbs.
He is not altogether dead, he is lost.
And although we may close the doors, he insists.

Now I remember the dead of my own house.
Faces lost in my head today, the faces
eyeless, or with eyes that are staring, emptied,
Am I perhaps searching in them for my secret,
the god of blood who excites the blood in me,
the god of ice, the god who devours me?
Their silence is the mirror of my life
in my own life their death is continuing:
among their mistakes, I am the last mistake.

Now I remember the dead of my own house.
The treacherous circle of imagining
that always flows out into its starting-place,
saliva that is dust, is dust and ashes,
the lying of the mouth and the lie itself,

el mal sabor del mundo, el impasible,
abstracto abismo del espejo a solas,
todo lo que al morir quedó en espera,
todo lo que no fue—y lo que fue
y ya no será más, en mí se alza,
pide, comer el pan, la fruta, el cuerpo,
beber el agua que le fue negada.
Pero no hay agua ya, todo está seco,
no sabe el pan, la fruta amarga,
amor domesticado, masticado,
en jaulas de barrotes invisibles
mono onanista y perra amaestrada,
lo que devoras te devora,
tu víctima también es tu verdugo.
Montón de días muertos, arrugados
periódicos, y noches descorchadas
y amaneceres, corbata, nudo corredizo:
"*saluda al sol, araña, no seas rencorosa ...*"

Es un desierto circular el mundo,
el cielo está cerrado y el infierno vacío.

the bad taste of the world, the indifferent,
abstract abyss of a mirror, nothing else,
all that which at the point of death is waiting,
all that never was—whatever was
and now will never be, in me it rises
and begs the body, to eat bread, eat fruit,
and drink the water that it has been denied.
But now there is no water, everything's dry,
bread has no taste, and fruit is bitter,
love is domesticated, masticated,
caged up within invisible prison bars,
masturbating ape and well-trained bitch,
what you devour is devouring you,
your victim is your executioner.
A heap of dead days, crumpled-up
newspapers, nights decorticated
and daybreaks, a tie, a running knot:
"*greet the sun, spider, and not in rancor ...*"

This world is a desert that is a circle,
heaven is closed and hell is empty.

Hacia el poema

I

Palabras, ganancias, de un cuarto de hora arrancado al árbol calcinado del lenguaje, entre los buenos días y las buenas noches, puertas de entrada y salida y entrada de un corredor que va de ningunaparte a ningúnlado.

Damos vueltas y vueltas en el vientre animal, en el vientre mineral, en el vientre temporal. Encontrar la salida: el poema.

Obstinación de ese rostro donde se quiebran mis mirados. Frente armada, invicta ante un paisaje en ruinas, tras el asalto al secreto. Melancolía de volcán.

La benévola jeta de piedra de cartón del Jefe, del Conductor, fetiche del siglo; los yo, tú, él, tejedores de tela de araña, pronombres armados de uñas; las divinidades sin rostro, abstractas. Él y nosotros, Nosotros y Él: nadie y ninguno. Dios padre se venga en todos estos ídolos.

El instante se congela, blancura compacta que ciega y no responde y se desvanece, témpano empujado por corrientes circulares. Ha de volver.

Arrancar la máscaras de la fantasía, clavar una pica en el centro sensible: provocar la erupción.

Cortar el cordón umbilical, matar bien a la Madre: crimen que el poeta moderno cometió por todos, en nombre de todos. Toca al nuevo poeta descubrir a la Mujer.

Toward the poem

(STARTING—POINTS)

I

Words, the profit of a quarter hour pulled from the burnt-out tree of language, between the good mornings and good nights, the way in and the way out and the way in of a corridor going from noplace to nowhere.

We turn and turn in the animal belly, in the mineral belly, in the belly of time. To find the way out: the poem.

Obstinacy of that face where my gaze is stopped. Armed forehead, unconquered before a ruined countryside, after besieging the secret. Volcanic melancholy.

Benevolent snout of the Leader, the Boss, the century's fetish; the I, you, he, spinners of spider-webs; pronouns whose weapons are fingernails; faceless divinities, abstractions. He and we, We and He: nobody and none. God the father avenges himself in all these idols.

The moment freezes, a compact whiteness that strikes us blind and makes no response and then dissolves, an iceberg carried by circular currents. It will be back.

Rip off the masks of fantasy, spike the living center: provoke the eruption.

Cut the umbilical cord, kill off the Mother: crime that the modern poet has committed for all, in the name of all. It is up to the new poet to discover Woman.

Hablar por hablar, arrancar sones a la desesperada, escribir al dictado lo que dice el vuelo de la mosca, ennegrecer. El tiempo se abre en dos: hora del salto mortal.

II

Palabras, frases, sílabas, astros que giran alrededor de un centro fijo. Dos cuerpos, muchos seres que se encuentran en una palabra. El papel se cubre de letras indelebles, que nadie dijo, que nadie dictó, que han caído allí y arden y queman y se apagan. Así pues, existe la poesía, el amor existe. Y si yo no existo, existes tú.

El chorro de agua. La bocanada de salud. Una muchacha reclinada sobre su pasado. El vino, el fuego, la guitarra, la sobremesa. Un muro de terciopelo rojo en una plaza de pueblo. Las aclamaciones, la caballería reluciente entrando a la ciudad, el pueblo en vilo: ¡himnos! La irrupción de lo blanco, de lo verde, de lo llameante. Lo demasiado fácil, lo que se escribe solo: la poesía.

El poema prepara un orden amoroso. Preveo un hombre—sol y una mujer-luna, el uno libre de su poder, la otra libre de su esclavitud, y amores implacables rayando el espacio negro. Todo ha de ceder a esas águilas incandescentes.

Por las almenas de tu frente el canto alborea. La justicia poética incendia campos de oprobio: no hay sitio para la nostalgia, el yo, el nombre propio.

Todo poema se cumple a expensas del poeta.

Mediodía futuro, árbol inmenso de follaje invisible. En las plazas cantan los hombres y las mujeres el canto solar, surtidor de transparencias. Me cubre la marejada amarilla: nada mío ha de hablar por mi boca.

Cuando la Historia duerme, habla en sueños: en la frente del pueblo dormido el poema es una constelación de sangre. Cuando la Historia despierta, la imagen se hace acto, acontece el poema: la poesía entra en acción.

Merece lo que sueñas.

Speak for the sake of speaking, force sounds out of the woman in despair, write from dictation what the flight of the fly dictates, blacken. Time opens in two: the hour of the somersault.

II

Words, phrases, syllables, stars turning about a fixed center. Two bodies, many beings meeting in one word. The paper becomes covered with indelible letters, spoken by nobody, dictated by nobody, that burn and flame up and go out. This, then, is how poetry exists, how love exists. And if I do not exist, you do.

The gush. A mouthful of health. A girl lying on her past. Wine, fire, guitar, tablecloth. A red plush wall in a village square. Cheers, glittering cavalry that enter the city, the people in flight: hymns! Eruption of white, green, fiery. The easiest thing, that which writes itself: poetry.

The poem prepares a loving order. I foresee a man sun and a moon woman, he free of his own power, she free of her slavery, and implacable love shining through black space. Everything must give way before these incandescent eagles.

On the battlements of your brow song finds its daybreak. Poetic justice sets fire to fields of shame: no place for nostalgia, for the I, the proper noun.

Every poem is made at the poet's expense.

Future noon, an immense tree of invisible leaves. In the streets, men and women singing the song of the sun, a fountain of transparencies. Yellow surf covers me: nothing of myself is to speak through my own mouth.

When History sleeps, it speaks in dreams: on the brow of the sleeping people, the poem is a constellation of blood. When History wakes, image becomes deed, the poem is achieved: poetry goes into action.

Deserve your dream.

Virgen

I

Ella cierra los ojos y en su adentro
está desnuda y niña, al pie del árbol.
Reposan a su sombra el tigre, el toro.
Tres corderos de bruma le da al tigre,
tres palomas al toro, sangre y plumas.
Ni plegarias de humo quiere el tigre
ni palomas el toro: *a ti te quieren.*
Y vuelan las palomas, vuela el toro,
y ella también, desnuda vía láctea,
vuela en un cielo visceral, oscuro.
Un maligno puñal ojos de gato
y amarillentas alas de petate
la sigue entre los aires. Y ella lucha
y vence a la serpiente, vence al águila,
y sobre el cuerno de la luna asciende ...

II

Por los espacios gira la doncella.
Nubes errantes, torbellinos, aire.
El cielo es una boca que bosteza,
boca de tiburón en donde ríen,
afilados relámpagos, los astros.
Vestida de azucena ella se acerca
y le arranca los dientes al dormido
y al aire sin edades los arroja:
islas que parpadean cayeron las estrellas,

Virgin

She closes her eyes and within her own self
is naked, a little girl, at the foot of the tree.
In her own shadow rest the tiger and the bull.
Three lambs of mist she offers to the tiger,
three doves to the bull, in all their blood and feathers.
The tiger does not want supplications of smoke
nor the bull feathers: it is you they want.
And the doves fly away, the bull flies over,
and she also, a naked milky way,
she flies across a visceral dark sky.
A maleficent dagger with cat's eyes,
rattan-mat wings a little yellowing,
follows her through the winds. She struggles,
defeats the serpent and defeats the eagle
and over the horn of the moon she ascends ...

II

Among the spaces the young girl turns,
Wandering clouds, whirlwinds, air.
The whole sky is a mouth that yawns,
a shark's mouth open, laughter of
those sharpened lightnings, stars.
Clothed in lilies, she comes near
and while he sleeps, she pulls his teeth
and hurls them into ageless air:
blinking islands, the stars fallen down,

cayó al mantel la sal desparramada,
lluvia de plumas fue la garza herida,
se quebró la guitarra y el espejo
también, como la luna, cayó en trizas.
Y la estatua cayó. Viriles miembros
se retorcieron en el polvo, vivos.

III

Rocas y mar. El sol envejecido
quema las piedras que la mar amarga.
Cielo de piedra. Mar de piedra. Nadie.
Arrodillada cava las arenas,
cava la piedra con las uñas rotas.
¿A qué desenterrar del polvo estatuas?
La boca de los muertos está muerta.
Sobre la alfombra junta las figuras
de su rompecabezas infinito.
Y siempre falta una, sólo una,
y nadie sabe dónde está, secreta.
En la sala platican las visitas.
El viento gime en el jardín en sombras.
Está enterrada al pie del árbol. ¿Quién?
La llave, la palabra, la sortija ...
Pero es muy tarde ya, todos se han ido,
su madre sola al pie de la escalera
es una llama que se desvanece
y crece la marea de lo oscuro
y borra los peldaños uno a uno
y se aleja el jardín y ella se aleja
en la noche embarcada ...

IV

Al pie del árbol otra vez. No hay nada:
latas, botellas rotas, un cuchillo,
los restos de un domingo ya oxidado.

the scattered salt falls on the cloth,
the wounded heron in a rain of plumes,
the guitar breaks, the glass breaks,
mirror and moon in their fragments down.
And the statue fallen. Its virile limbs
twist and writhe in the dust, alive.

III

Rocks and the sea. The sun in its old age
burns up the rocks embittered by the sea.
Sky of stone, Sea of stone. No one.
Down on her knees, she is digging at the sand,
digging the stone out with her broken nails.
Why dig statues out of dust?
The mouth of the dead is dead.
On the carpet, she joins the figures of
an infinite puzzle of dismemberment.
And always one missing, always only one,
and no one knows where this one can be hidden.
The talk of visitors in the drawing room,
the whining of the wind in the shadowed garden.
Buried deep at the foot of the tree. Which?
The key, the word, the ring ...
But it is too late now, everyone is gone,
only her mother at the foot of the staircase
is there, she is a flame that vanishes
and the tide of darkness rises
and erases one by one the rising stairs
and the garden withdraws and she withdraws
sailing into the night ...

IV

At the foot of the tree again. There is nothing here:
a few cans, broken bottles, and a knife,
the remains of a Sunday that is rusty now.

Muge el toro sansón, herido y solo
por los sinfines de la noche en ruinas
y por los prados amarillos rondan
el león calvo, el tigre despintado.
Ella se aleja del jardín desierto
y por calles lluviosas llega a casa.
Llama, mas nadie le contesta; avanza
y no hay nadie detrás de cada puerta
y va de nadie a puerta hasta que llega
a la última puerta, la tapiada,
Busca la llave pero se ha perdido,
la golpea, la araña, la golpea,
durante siglos la golpea
y la puerta es más alta a cada siglo
y más cerrada y puerta a cada golpe.
Ella ya no la alcanza y sólo aguarda
sentada en su sillita que alguien abra:
Señor, abre las puertas de tu nube,
abre tus cicatrices mal cerradas,
llueve sobre mis senos arrugados,
llueve sobre los huesos y las piedras,
que tu semilla rompa la corteza,
la costra de mi sangre endurecida.
Devuélveme a la noche del Principio,
de tu costado desprendida sea
planeta opaco que tu luz enciende.

Berkeley, 1944

Bellowing of the bull Samson, alone
and wounded in the endlessness of night's ruins
and ranging over the yellow countryside
the maneless lion, the disfigured tiger.
She has gone out of the deserted garden,
by rainy avenues reaches the house.
She rings, but no one answers; she goes through
and there is no one behind any door,
she goes from nobody to the door, and she reaches
the final door, the one that is walled-up,
She looks for the key but she has lost the key,
she knocks, she claws at it, she knocks,
for centuries she knocks
and every century the door is higher,
a more locked door at each knock.
She is no longer trying, but simply waiting,
sitting in her little chair, until someone opens it:
Lord, open the doors of your cloud,
open the scars of your wounds barely closed,
rain your rain down on my wrinkled breasts,
rain down on the bones and on the stones,
let your seed come and break the rind,
the hardened crust of my blood.
Take me back to the night of Origin,
and from your side let me be taken out
an opaque planet on fire with your light.

El prisionero

(HOMENAJE Á D.A.F. DE SADE)

> *a fin que ... les traces de ma tombe disparaissent de dessus*
> *la surface de la terre comme je me flatte que ma mémoire*
> *s'effacera de l'esprit des hommes ...*
>
> Testamento de Sade

No te has desvanecido.
Las letras de tu nombre son todavía una cicatriz que no se cierra,
un tatuaje de infamia sobre ciertas frentes.

Cometa de pesada y rutilante cola dialéctica,
atraviesas el siglo diecinueve con una granada de verdad en
    la mano
y estallas al llegar a nuestra época.

Máscara que sonríe bajo un antifaz rosa,
hecho de párpados de ajusticiado,
verdad partida en mil pedazos de fuego,
¿qué quieren decir todos esos fragmentos gigantescos,
esa manada de icebergs que zarpan de tu pluma y en alta mar
    enfilan hacia costas sin nombre,
esos delicados instrumentos de cirugía para extirpar el chancro
    de Dios,
esos aullidos que interrumpen tus majestuosos razonamientos
    de elefante,
esas repeticiones atroces de relojería descompuesta,
toda esa oxidada herramienta de tortura?

El erudito y el poeta,
el sabio, el literato, el enamorado,

The prisoner

(HOMAGE TO D.A.F. DE SADE)

> *a fin que ... les traces de ma tombe disparaissent de dessus*
> *la surface de la terre comme je me flatte que ma mémoire*
> *s'effacera de l'esprit des hommes ...*
>
> Testament of Sade

You have not disappeared.
The letters of your name are still a scar that will not heal,
the tattoo of disgrace on certain faces.

Comet whose body is substance, whose tail glitters in dialectics,
you rush through the nineteenth century holding a grenade
   of truth,
exploding as you come to our own time.

A mask that smiles beneath a veil of pink
made of the eyelids of the executed,
truth broken into a thousand flames of fire.
What do they mean, those giant fragments,
that herd of icebergs sailing from your pen and from the high
   seas heading toward the nameless coasts?
those delicate surgical instruments made for cutting away the
   chancre of God?
those howls interrupting your kingly
   elephant thoughts?
the frightful striking of out-of-order clocks?
all of that rusty armament of torture?

The learned man and the poet,
the scholar, the writer, the lover,

el maníaco y el que sueña en la abolición de nuestra
    siniestra realidad,
disputan como perros sobre los restos de tu obra.
Tú, que estabas contra todos,
eres ahora un nombre, un jefe, una bandera.

Inclinado sobre la vida como Saturno sobre sus hijos,
recorres con fija mirada amorosa
los surcos calcinados que dejan el semen, la sangre y la lava.
Los cuerpos, frente a frente como astros feroces,
están hechos de la misma sustancia de los soles.
Lo que llamamos amor o muerte, libertad o destino,
¿no se llama catástrofe, no se llama hecatombe?
¿Dónde están las fronteras entre espasmo y terremoto,
entre erupción y cohabitación?

Prisionero en tu castillo de cristal de roca
cruzas galerías, cámaras, mazmorras,
vastos patios donde la vid se enrosca a columnas solares,
graciosos cementerios donde danzan los chopos inmóviles.
Muros, objetos, cuerpos te repiten.
¡Todo es espejo!
Tu imagen te persigue.

El hombre está habitado por silencio y vacío.
¿Cómo saciar esta hambre,
cómo acallar este silencio y poblar su vacío?
¿Cómo escapar a mi imagen?
Sólo en mi semejante me trasciendo,
sólo su sangre da fe de otra existencia.
Justina solo vive por Julieta,
las víctimas engendran los verdugos.
El cuerpo que hoy sacrificamos
¿no es el Dios que mañana sacrifica?

La imaginación es la espuela del deseo,
su reino es inagotable e infinito como el fastidio,
su reverso y gemelo.

the maniac and the man who dreams the destruction of our
    perverse reality,
they fight like dogs over the bones of your work.
You who stood against all of them,
you are today a name, a leader, a banner.

Bending over life like Saturn over his sons
you scan with your steady look of love
the whitened ridges left by semen, blood, lava.
These bodies, face to face like blazing stars,
are made of the same substance as the suns.
We call this love or death; liberty or doom.
Is it catastrophe? Is it the grave of man?
Where is the borderline between spasm and earthquake,
eruption and coitus?

Prisoner in your castle of crystal of rock
you pass through dungeons, chambers and galleries,
enormous courts whose vines twist on sunny pillars,
seductive graveyards where the still black poplars dance.
Walls, things, bodies, reflecting you.
All is mirror!
Your image persecutes you.

Man is inhabited by silence and by space.
How can this hunger be met and satisfied?
How can you still the silence? How can the void be peopled?
How can my image ever be escaped?
Only in my likeness can I transcend myself
the other's existence affirmed by his blood alone.
Justine is alive only through Juliette,
the victims breed their executioners.
This body which today we sacrifice,
is it not the god who tomorrow will sacrifice?

Imagination is desire's spur,
territory is endless, infinite as boredom,
its opposite and twin.

Muerte o placer, inundación o vómito,
otoño parecido al caer de los días,
volcán o sexo,
soplo, verano que incendia las cosechas,
astros o colmillos,
petrificada cabellera del espanto,
espuma roja del deseo, matanza en alta mar,
rocas azules del delirio,
formas, imágenes, burbujas, hambre de ser,
eternidades momentáneas,
desmesuras: tu medida de hombre.
Atrévete:
la libertad es la elección de la necesidad.
Sé el arco y la flecha, la cuerda y el ay.
El sueño es explosivo. Estalla. Vuelve a ser sol.

En tu castillo de diamente tu imagen se destroza y se rehace,
   infatigable.

Aviñon, 1948

Pleasure or death, vomit or flooding in,
autumn, resembling the going down of day,
sex or volcano,
a gust of wind, summer that sets the fields on fire,
eye-teeth or stars,
the stony hair of dread,
red foam of desire, slaughter on the high seas,
and the blue rocks of delirium,
forms, images, gurgles, and the rage for life,
eternities in flashes,
excesses: your measure of a man.
Now dare:
freedom is willingness toward necessity.
Be the arrow, the bow, the chord and the cry.
Dream is explosive. It bursts. Become again sun.

In your diamond castle, your image destroys itself, remakes itself,
    tireless.

Himno entre ruinas

donde espumoso el mar siciliano ...
Góngora

Coronado de sí el día extiende sus plumas.
¡Alto grito amarillo,
caliente surtidor en el centro de un cielo
imparcial y benéfico!
Las apariencias son hermosas en esta su verdad momentánea.
El mar trepa la costa,
se afianza entre las peñas, araña deslumbrante;
la herida cárdena del monte resplandece;
un puñado de cabras es un rebaño de piedras;
el sol pone su huevo de oro y se derrama sobre el mar.
Todos es dios.
¡Estatua rota,
columnas comidas por la luz,
ruinas vivas en un mundo de muertos en vida!

Cae la noche sobre Teotihuacán.
En lo alto de la pirámide los muchachos fuman marihuana,
suenan guitarras roncas.
¿Qué yerba, qué agua de vida ha de darnos la vida,
dónde desenterrar la palabra,
la proporción que rige al himno y al discurso,
al baile, a la ciudad y a la balanza?
El canto mexicano estalla en un carajo,
estrella de colores que se apaga,
piedra que nos cierra las puertas del contacto.
Sabe la tierra a tierra envejecida.

Hymn among the ruins

Where foams the Sicilian sea ...
Góngora

Self crowned the day displays its plumage.
A shout tall and yellow,
impartial and beneficent,
a hot geyser into the middle sky!
Appearances are beautiful in this their momentary truth.
The sea mounts the coast,
clings between the rocks, a dazzling spider;
the livid wound on the mountain glistens;
a handful of goats becomes a flock of stones;
the sun lays its gold egg upon the sea.
All is god.
A broken statue,
columns gnawed by the light,
ruins alive in a world of death in life!

Night falls on Teotihuacán.
On top of the pyramid the boys are smoking marijuana,
harsh guitars sound.
What weed, what living waters will give life to us,
where shall we unearth the word,
the relations that govern hymn and speech,
the dance, the city and the measuring scales?
The song of Mexico explodes in a curse,
a colored star that is extinguished,
a stone that blocks our doors of contact.
Earth tastes of rotten earth.

Los ojos ven, las manos tocan.
Bastan aquí unas cuantas cosas:
tuna, espinoso planeta coral,
higos encapuchados,
uvas con gusto a resurrección,
almejas, virginidades ariscas,
sal, queso, vino, pan solar.
Desde lo alto de su morenía una isleña me mira,
esbelta catedral vestida de luz.
Torres de sal, contra los pinos verdes de la orilla
surgen las velas blancas de las barcas.
La luz crea templos en el mar.

Nueva York, Londres, Moscú.
La sombra cubre al llano con su yedra fantasma,
con su vacilante vegetación de escalofrío,
su vello ralo, su tropel de ratas.
A trechos tirita un sol anémico.
Acodado en montes que ayer fueron ciudades,
    Polifemo bosteza.
Abajo, entre los hoyos, se arrastra un rebaño de hombres.

Ver, tocar formas hermosas, diarias.
Zumba la luz, dardos y alas.
Huele a sangre la mancha de vino en el mantel.
Como el coral sus ramas en el agua
extiendo mis sentidos en la hora viva:
el instante se cumple en una concordancia amarilla,
¡oh mediodía, espiga henchida de minutos,
copa de eternidad!

Mis pensamientos se bifurcan, serpean, se enredan,
recomienzan,
y al fin se inmovilizan, ríos que no desembocan,
delta de sangre bajo un sol sin crepúsculo.
¿Y todo ha de parar en este chapoteo de aguas muertas?

Eyes see, hands touch.
Here a few things suffice:
prickly pear, coral and thorny planet,
the hooded figs,
grapes that taste of the resurrection,
clams, stubborn maidenheads,
salt, cheese, wine, the sun's bread.
An island girl looks on me from the height of her duskiness,
a slim cathedral clothed in light.
A tower of salt, against the green pines of the shore,
the white sails of the boats arise.
Light builds temples on the sea.

New York, London, Moscow.
Shadow covers the plain with its phantom ivy,
with its swaying and feverish vegetation,
its mousy fur, its rats swarm.
Now and then an anemic sun shivers.
Propping himself on mounts that yesterday were cities,
    Polyphemus yawns.
Below, among the pits, a herd of men dragging along.
Until lately people considered them unclean animals.

To see, to touch each day's lovely forms.
The light throbs, all darties and wings.
The wine-stain on the tablecloth smells of blood.
As the coral thrusts branches into the water
I stretch my senses to this living hour:
the moment fulfills itself in a yellow harmony.
Midday, ear of wheat heavy with minutes,
eternity's brimming cup.

My thoughts are split, meander, grow entangled,
start again,
and finally lose headway, endless rivers,
delta of blood beneath an unwinking sun.
And must everything end in this spatter of stagnant water?

¡Día, redondo día,
luminosa naranja de veinticuatro gajos,
todos atravesados por una misma y amarilla dulzura!
La inteligencia al fin encarna,
se reconcilian las dos mitades enemigas
y la conciencia-espejo se licúa,
vuelve a ser fuente, manantial de fábulas:
Hombre, árbol de imágenes,
palabras que son flores que son frutos que son actos.

Nápoles, 1948

Day, round day,
shining orange with four-and-twenty bars,
all one single yellow sweetness!
Mind embodies in forms,
the two hostile become one,
the conscience-mirror liquifies,
once more a fountain of legends:
man, tree of images,
words which are flowers become fruits which are deeds.

[W.C.W.]

Máscaras del alba

Sobre el tablero de la plaza
se demoran la últimas estrellas.
Torres de luz y alfiles afilados
cercan las monarquías espectrales,
¡Vano ajedrez, ayer combate de ángeles!

Fulgor de agua estancada donde flotan
pequeñas alegrías ya verdosas,
la manzana podrida de un deseo,
un rostro recomido por la luna,
el minuto arrugado de una espera,
todo lo que la vida no consume,
los restos del festín de la impaciencia.

Abre los ojos el agonizante.
Esa brizna de luz que tras cortinas
espía al que la expía entre estertores
es la mirada que no mira y mira,
el ojo en que espejean las imágenes
antes de despeñarse, el precipicio
cristalino, la tumba de diamante:
es el espejo que devora espejos.

Olivia, la ojizarca que pulsaba,
las blancas manos entre cuerdas verdes,
el arpa de cristal de la cascada,
nada contra corriente hasta la orilla
del despertar: la cama, el haz de ropas,
las manchas hidrográficas del muro,

Masks of dawn

Over the chessboard of the piazza
the last stars linger on their way.
Castles of light and shimmering thin bishops
surround these spectral monarchies.
The empty game, yesterday's war of angels!

Brilliance of stagnant water whereon float
a few small joys, already green,
the rotten apple of desire,
a face nibbled in places by the moon,
the wrinkled minute of an eagerness,
everything life itself has not consumed,
leavings of the orgy of impatience.

The man in his death-struggle open his eyes.
That splinter of light that through the curtains spies
on the one expiating among the death-rattles
is the look which does not look but looks,
the eye in whom the images form and shine
before they are scattered, and the glassy
precipice, and the grave of diamond:
this is the mirror that devours mirrors.

Olivia, blue-eyed lightly-touching woman,
white hands between the greenness of the cords,
the harp of crystal of the waterfall,
she swims against the current to the shore
of waking: the bed, the heap of clothes,
the hydrographic stains upon the wall,

ese cuerpo sin nombre que a su lado
mastica profecías y rezongos
y la abominación del cielo raso.
Bosteza lo real sus naderías,
se repite en horrores desventrados.

El prisionero de sus pensamientos
teje y desteje su tejido a ciegas,
escarba sus heridas, deletrea
las letras de su nombre, las dispersa,
y ellas insisten en el mismo estrago:
se engastan en su nombre desgastado.
Va de sí mismo hacia sí mismo, vuelve,
en el centro de sí se para y grita
¿quién va? y el surtidor de su pregunta
abre su flor absorta, centellea,
silba en el tallo, dobla la cabeza,
y al fin, vertiginoso, se desploma
roto como la espada contra el muro.

La joven domadora de relámpagos
y la que se desliza sobre el filo
resplandeciente de la guillotina;
el señor que desciende de la luna
con un fragante ramo de epitafios;
la frígida que lima en el insomnio
el pedernal gastado de su sexo;
el hombre puro en cuya sien anida
el águila real, la cejijunta
voracidad de un pensamiento fijo;
el árbol de ocho brazos anudados
que el rayo del amor derriba, incendia
y carboniza en lechos transitorios;
el enterrado en vida con su pena;
la joven muerta que se prostituye
y regresa a su tumba al primer gallo;
la víctima que busca a su asesino;

that nameless body who beside her lies
chewing on prophecies and mutterings
and the abomination of the flat ceiling.
Reality gaping among its trifles
repeating itself in disemboweled horrors.

The prisoner of his imagining
weaves and unravels his weaving sightlessly,
scrapes at his scars, plays games
with the letters of his name, scatters them,
and then they insist on the same havoc,
set in the setting of his corroded name.
He goes from himself toward himself, he turns,
in the center of himself he stops and shouts
Who's there? and the fountain of his questioning
opens its amazed flower, glistens,
its stalk hisses, it bends its head,
and finally, in its dizziness collapses,
shattered like the sword against the wall.

A young girl, tamer of the lightning-bolt,
and the woman slipping away along under
the glittering fine edge of the guillotine;
the gentleman who from the moon descends
with a sweet-smelling branch of epitaphs;
the frigid sleepless woman sharpening
the wornout flint-stone of her sex;
the man of purity, within whose forehead
the golden eagle makes his nest,
the monomaniac hunger of obsession;
the tree that has eight interlocked branches
struck by the bolt of love, set on fire
and burned to ash in transitory beds;
the man buried in life among his grief;
the young dead woman who prostitutes herself
and goes back to her grave at the first cock;
the victim searching out his murderer;

el que perdío su cuerpo, el que su sombra,
el que huye de sí y el que se busca
y se persigue y no se encuentra, todos,
vivos muertos al borde del instante
se detienen suspensos. Duda el tiempo,
el día titubea.
                    Soñolienta
en su lecho de fango, abre los ojos
Venecia y se recuerda: ¡pabellones
y un alto vuelo que se petrifica!
esplendor anegado ...
Los caballos de bronce de San Marcos
cruzan arquitecturas que vacilan,
descienden verdinegros hasta el agua
y se arrojan al mar, hacia Bizancio.

Oscilan masas de estupor y piedra,
mientras los pocos vivos de esta hora ...
Pero la luz avanza a grandes pasos,
aplastando bostezos y agonías.
¡Júbilos, resplandores que desgarran!
El alba lanza su primer cuchillo.

Venecia, 1948

he who has lost his body, and he his shadow,
he who escapes himself and he who hunts himself,
who pursues himself and never finds himself, all those,
the living corpses on the edge of the moment,
wait suspended. Time itself in doubt,
day hesitates.
                    Moving in dream,
upon her bed of mire and water, Venice
opens her eyes and remembers: canopies,
and a high soaring that has turned to stone!
Splendor flooded over ...
The bronze horses of San Marco
pass wavering architecture,
go down in their green darkness to the water
and throw themselves in the sea, toward Byzantium.

Volumes of stupor and stone, back and forth
in this hour among the few alive ...
But the light advances in great strides,
shattering yawns and agonies.
Exultance, radiances that tear apart!
Dawn throws its first knife.

Fuente

El mediodía alza en vilo al mundo.
Y las piedras donde el viento borra lo que a ciegas escribe
    el tiempo,
las torres que al caer la tarde inclinan la frente,
la nave que hace siglos encalló en la roca, la iglesia de oro que
    tiembla al peso de una cruz de palo,
las plazas donde si un ejército acampa se siente desamparado y
    sin defensa,
el fuerte que hinca la rodilla ante la luz que irrumpe por la loma,
los parques y el corro cuchicheante de los olmos y los álamos,
las columnas y los arcos a la medida exacta de la gloria,
la muralla que abierta al sol dormita, echada sobre sí misma,
    sobre su propia hosquedad desplomada,
el rincón visitado sólo por los misántropos que rondan las afueras:
    el pino y el sauce,
los mercados bajo el fuego graneado de los gritos,
el muro a media calle, que nadie sabe quién edificó ni con qué
    fin, el desollado, el muro en piedra viva,
todo lo atado al suelo por amor de materia enamorada,
    rompe amarras
y asciende entre las manos de esta hora.

El viejo mundo de las piedras se levanta y vuela.
Es un pueblo de ballenas y delfines que retozan en pleno cielo,
    arrojándose grandes chorros de gloria;
y los cuerpos de piedra, arrastrados por el lento huracán de calor,
escurren luz y entre las nubes relucen, gozosos.
La ciudad lanza sus cadenas al río y vacía de sí misma,
de su carga de sangre, de su carga de tiempo, reposa
hecha un ascua, hecha un sol en el centro del torbellino.
El presente la mece.

Fountain

Noonday raises a world in flight.
And the stones where wind wipes out all that gropingly
    time writes,
towers that bend their heads with falling afternoon,
the ark that centuries ago ran aground on the rock, the golden
    church wavering under the weight of a cross of sticks,
plazas where an army encamped feels helpless,
    defenseless,
the fortress who kneels before light irrupting through the foothills,
the parks and the whispered syllables of elms and willows,
pillars and arches to the exact measure of glory,
the drowsy wall that opens to the sun, fallen down on itself,
    collapsed of its own arrogance,
the corner visited only by misanthropes who walk the suburbs:
    the pine and the poplar,
markets under the drumfire of shouts,
the wall in the middle of the street, built no-one knows why, meant
    to end no-one knows where, ruined, the wall of living stones,
everything bound to earth for love of matter in love
    breaks bounds
and rises in the hands of this hour.

The old world of stones rises in flight.
It is a tribe of whales and dolphins that play in full sky, throwing
    one another great spouts of glory;
and the bodies of stone, dragged by the slow hurricane of light,
drip light, and in delight among the clouds they glitter.
The city hurls its chains into the river and emptied of itself,
its burden of blood, its burden of time, it rests
transformed into a live coal, a sun in a whirlwind.
The present is rocking it.

Todo es presencia, todos los siglos son este Presente.
¡Ojo feliz que ya no mira porque todo es presencia y su propia
    visión fuera de sí lo mira!
¡Hunde la mano, coge el fulgor, el pez solar, la llama entre
    lo azul,
el canto que se mece en el fuego del día!
Y la gran ola vuelve y me derriba, echa a volar la mesa y los
    papeles y en lo alto de su cresta me suspende,
música detenida en su más, luz que no pestañea, ni cede,
    ni avanza.
Todos es presente, espejos sin revés: no hay sombra, no hay lado
    opaco, todo es ojo,
todo es presencia, estoy presente en todas partes y para ver mejor,
    para mejor arder, me apago
y caigo en mí y salgo de mí y subo hasta el cohete y bajo hasta
    el hachazo
porque la gran esfera, la gran bola de tiempo incandescente,
el fruto que acumula todos los jugos de la historia, la presencia,
    el presente, estalla
como un espejo roto al mediodía, como un mediodía roto contra
    el mar y la sal.

Toco la piedra y no contesta, cojo la llama y no me quema,
    ¿qué esconde esta presencia?
No hay nada atrás, las raíces están quemadas, podridos
    los cimientos,
basta un manotazo para echar abajo esta grandeza.
¿Y quién asume la grandeza si nadie asume el desamparo?
Penetro en mi oquedad: yo no respondo, no me doy
    la cara,
perdí el rostro después de haber perdido cuerpo y alma.
Y mi vida desfila ante mis ojos sin que uno solo de mis actos lo
    reconozca mío:
¿y el delirio de hacer saltar la muerte con el apenas golpe de alas
    de una imagen

All is presence, all the centuries are this Present.
Happy the eye which no longer looks, for all is presence and its
  own vision from outside itself looks at it!
The hand plunges, it grasps the brilliance, the solar fish, the
  flame in that blue,
the song that is rocking in the fire of day!
And the great wave turns and throws me down, it scatters the
  table and the papers and it suspends me from the top of its crest,
music is at its most, light unwinking, unyielding,
  unmoving.
All is present, mirror without a back: there is no shadow, no
  opaque side, all is eye,
all is presence, everywhere I am present and to see better, to
  burn better, I die out
and fall into myself and cease as myself and rise with the rocket
  and drop with the axe-blow
because the great sphere, that incandescent and great ball of time,
that fruit that concentrates all the juices of history, the presence,
  the present, bursts
like a mirror broken at noonday, like a noonday broken on salt
  and the sea.

I touch the stone, it does not answer, I grasp the flame, it does
  not burn me,—what does this presence hide?
There is nothing behind, the roots are parched, the foundation
  now powder,
one slap would do to bring low this greatness.
Who will assume the greatness if no-one assumes the helplessness?
Entering into my hollowness: I don't respond, I don't face up
  to myself,
I lost face after I lost body and soul.
And my life passes before my eyes without my recognizing one
  of my acts as mine:
—and the rapture of having made death jump with barely a
  wingblow of an image

y la larga noche pasada en esculpir el instantáneo cuerpo del
    relámpago
y la noche de amor puente colgante entre esta vida y
    la otra?

No duele la antigua herida, no arde la vieja quemadura, es una
    cicatriz casi borrada
el sitio de la separación, el lugar del desarraigo, la boca por donde
    hablan en sueños la muerte y la vida
es una cicatriz invisible.
Yo no daría la vida por mi vida: es otra mi verdadera historia.

La ciudad sigue en pie.
Tiembla en la luz, hermosa.
Se posa el sol en su diestra pacífica.
Son más altos, más blancos, los chorros de las fuentes.
Todo se pone en pie para caer mejor.
Y el caído bajo el hacha de su propio delirio se levanta.
De su frente hendida brota un último pájaro.
Es el doble de sí mismo,
el joven que cada cien años vuelve a decir unas palabras, siempre
    las mismas,
la columna transparente que un instante se oscurece y otro
    centellea,
según avanza la veloz escritura del destino.
En el centro de la plaza la rota cabeza del poeta es una fuente.
La fuente canta para todos.

Aviñon, 1950

and the long night spent in sculpturing the sudden body of
  lightning
and the night of love, a swinging bridge between this life and
  the other?

The ancient wound does not hurt, the old burn does not sting,
  the scar is nearly obliterated
of the place of separation, the point of expulsion, the mouth
  through which death and life speak in their sleep
is now an invisible scar.
I would not give life for my life: my true story is otherwise.

The city is up and alert.
It is lovely, it quivers in the sun.
The sun comes to rest on its peaceful right hand.
The jets of the fountains are taller, whiter.
Everything stands tall to make a finer fall.
And he who has fallen under the axe of his own wildness gets up.
From his split forehead bursts one last bird.
He is his own double,
the young man who every century says a few words again, always
  the same words,
the clear pillar which at one moment darkens and at the next
  glitters,
advancing with the swift hand of destiny as it writes.
In the center of the plaza the broken head of the poet is a fountain.
The fountain sings for all.

Repaso nocturno

Toda la noche batalló con la noche,
ni vivo ni muerto,
a tientas penetrando en su sustancia,
llenándose hasta el borde de sí mismo.

Primero fue el extenderse en lo oscuro,
hacerse inmenso en lo inmenso,
reposar en el centro insondable del reposo.
Fluía el tiempo, fluía su ser,
fluían en una sola corriente indivisible.
A zarpazos somnolientos el agua caía y se levantaba,
se despeñaban alma y cuerpo, pensamiento y huesos:
¿pedía redención el tiempo,
pedía el agua erguirse, pedía verse,
vuelta transparente monumento de su caída?
Río arriba, donde lo no formado empieza,
al agua se desplomaba con los ojos cerrados.
Volvía el tiempo a su origen, manándose.

Allá, del otro lado, un fulgor le hizo señas.
Abrió los ojos, se encontró en la orilla:
ni vivo ni muerto,
al lado de su cuerpo abandonado.
Empezó el asedio de los signos,
la escritura de sangre de la estrella en el cielo,
las ondas concéntricas que levanta una frase
al caer y caer en la conciencia.
Ardió su frente cubierta de inscripciones,
santo y señas súbitos abrieron laberintos y espesuras,
cambiaron reflejos tácitos los cuatro puntos cardinales.

The middle of the night

All of the night in conflict with the night,
neither alive nor dead,
groping, penetrating its substance,
pouring in up to the brim of himself.

At first, there was the extending into the dark,
making himself immense in the immense,
coming to rest in the unsoundable center of rest.
Time flowed, his being flowed,
they flowed in one single indivisible current.
In sleep-heavy paw-strokes the water fell and rose,
soul, body plummeted, thought and bones:
was it time, begging for redemption,
was water begging to be erect, begging to see itself,
become a transparent monument to its fall?
Up river, where the unformed begins,
water leaned over and fell, his eyes were closed.
Time returned to its origin, flowing out.

Far out, on the other side, a blaze signalled to him.
He opened his eyes, found himself on the shore:
neither alive nor dead,
beside his abandoned body.
Then began the siege of signals,
the star's writing on the sky in blood,
concentric circles by a sentence lifted
falling and falling in consciousness.
His head on fire, covered with inscriptions,
unforeseen passwords opened mazes and densities,
silent mirrors transformed the four directions.

Su pensamiento mismo, entre los obeliscos derribado,
fue piedra negra tatuada por el rayo.
Pero el sueño no vino.

¡Ciega batalla de alusiones,
oscuro cuerpo a cuerpo con el tiempo sin cuerpo!
Cayó de rostro en rostro,
                              de año en año,
hasta el primer vagido:
                              humus de vida,
tierra que se destierra,
                              cuerpo que se desnace,
vivo para le muerte,
                              muerto para la vida.

(*A esta hora hay mediadores en todas partes,*
hay puentes invisibles entre el dormir y el velar.
Los dormidos muerden el racimo de su propia fatiga,
el racimo solar de la resurrección cotidiana;
los desvelados tallan el diamante que ha de vencer a la noche;
aun los que están solos llevan en sí su pareja encarnizada,
en cada espejo yace un doble,
un adversario que nos refleja y nos abisma;   ·
el fuego precioso oculto bajo la capa de seda negra,
el vampiro ladrón dobla la esquina y desaparece, ligero,
robado por su propia ligereza;
con el peso de su acto a cuestas
se precipita en su dormir sin sueño el asesino,
ya para siempre a solas, sin el otro;
abandonados a la corriente todopoderosa,
flor doble que brota de un tallo único,
los enamorados cierran los ojos en lo alto del beso:
la noche se abre para ellos y les devuelve lo perdido,
las palabras dormidas en los labios del agua, en la frente del árbol,
   en el pecho del monte,
el vino negro en la copa hecha de una sola gota de sol,
la visión doble, la mariposa fija por un instante en el centro
   del cielo,
en el ala derecha un grano de luz y en la izquierda uno de sombra.
Reposa la ciudad en los hombros del obrero dormido,
la semilla del canto se abre en la frente del poeta.)

His thought itself, torn down among obelisks,
was black stone tattooed by lightning-stroke.
But sleep did not come.

Blind battle of allusions,
dark hand-to-hand combat against handless time!
He fell from face to face,
                         from year to year,
to the first newborn cry:
                         humus of life,
land that strips itself,
                         body again unborn,
alive to death,
             dead to life.

(*At this time there are mediators everywhere,
there are invisible bridges between sleep and waking.
The sleepers bite the grapes of tiredness,
the solar cluster of daily resurrection;
the sleepless are cutting the diamond that is to conquer night;
even the lonely ones bear in themselves their carnivorous twin,
in every mirror lies a double,
an adversary who reflects us and humbles us;
the precious fire hidden under the black silk cloak,
the robber vampire turns the corner and vanishes, nimbly,
thieved by his own agility;
with the weight of his act on his own shoulders
the assassin dives into his dreamless sleep,
now he is alone forever, without the other;
abandoned now to the all-powerful current,
a double flower sprung from a single stalk,
the lovers close their eyes in the depth of the kiss:
for them, night opens and restores the loss,
words asleep on the lips of water, in the head of the tree, in the
    breast of the mountain,
the black wine in the cup made of one drop of sun,
vision doubles, the butterfly holds still for a moment at the center of
    the sky,
on its right wing a grain of light and, on its left, one of shadow.
The city rests on the shoulder of the sleeping worker,
the seed of the song opens in the head of the poet.*)

El escorpión ermitaño en la sombra se aguza.
Noche en entredicho,
instante que balbucea y no acaba de decir lo que quiere:
¿Saldrá mañana el sol,
se anega el astro en su luz,
se ahoga en su cólera fija?
¿Cómo decir buenos días a la vida?
No preguntes más,
no hay nada que decir, nada tampoco que callar.
El pensamiento brilla, se apaga, vuelve,
idéntico a sí mismo se devora y engendra, se repite,
ni vivo ni muerto,
en torno siempre al ojo frío que lo piensa.

Volvió a su cuerpo, se metió en sí mismo.
Y el sol tocó la frente del insomne,
brusca victoria de un espejo que no refleja ya
    ninguna imagen.

Paris, 1950

The eremite scorpion sharpens himself in the shadow.
Nocturnal interdict,
Moment that stammers and never finishes its meaning:
Will the sun rise tomorrow?
Does the star drown in its light,
go down in its rigid fury?
How do you say good morning to life?
Ask nothing more,
there is nothing to say, and nothing to conceal.
Thought shines, goes out, returns,
identical with itself it consumes itself and begets, recurs,
neither alive nor dead,
turning forever around the cold eye thinking it.

He returned to his body, he entered into himself.
And the sun touched his sleepless head,
an abrupt victory of a mirror that no longer reflects a
    single image.

Mutra (*Fragmento*)

Como una madre demasiado amorosa, una madre terrible
  que ahoga,
como una lenoa taciturna y solar,
como una sola ola del tamaño del mar,
ha llegado sin hacer ruido y en cada uno de nosotros se asienta
  como un rey
y los días de vidrio se derriten y en cada pecho erige un trono de
  espinas y de brasas
y su imperio es un hipo solemne, una aplastada respiración de
  dioses y animales de ojos dilatados
y bocas llenas de insectos calientes pronunciando una misma
  sílaba día y noche, día y noche.
¡Verano, boca inmensa, vocal hecha de vaho y jadeo!

Este día herido de muerte que se arrastra a lo largo del tiempo
  sin acabar de morir,
y el día que lo sigue y ya escarba impaciente la indecisa tierra
  del alba,
y los otros que esperan su hora en los vastos establos del año,
este día y sus cuatro cachorros, la mañana de cola de cristal y el
  mediodía con su ojo único,
el mediodía absorto en su luz, sentado en su esplendor,
la tarde rica en pájaros y la noche con sus luceros armados de
  punta en blanco,
este día y las presencias que alza o derriba el sol con un
  simple aletazo:
la muchacha que aparece en la plaza y es un chorro de
  frescura pausada,
el mendigo que se levanta como una flaca plegaria, montón de
  basura y cánticos gangosos,

Mutra (*Fragment*)

Like a too-loving mother, a terrible mother
   of suffocation,
like a silent lioness of sunlight,
a single wave the size of the sea,
it has arrived noiselessly and in each of us has taken its place like
   a king
and the glass days melt and in each breast is erected a throne of
   thorns and live coals
and its dominion is a solemn hiccup, a crushed breathing of gods
   and animals with eyes dilated
and mouths full of hot insects uttering one same syllable day and
   night, day and night.
Summer, enormous mouth, vowel made of fumes and panting!

This day wounded to death creeping along the length of time and
   never finished with dying,
and the day to come, now scraping impatiently at the no-man's-
   land of dawn,
and the rest waiting their hour in the vast stables of the year,
this day and its four pups, morning with its crystal tail and noon
   with its one eye,
noon absorbed in its light, seated in splendor,
afternoon rich in birds, night with its bright stars armed and in
   full regalia,
this day and the presences that the sun exalts or pulls down with
   a simple wingblow:
the girl who appears in the street and is a stream of
   quiet freshness,
the beggar raising himself up like a lean prayer, a heap of
   garbage and whining canticles,

las bugambilias rojas negras a fuerza de encarnadas, moradas de
tanto azul acumulado,
las mujeres albañiles que llevan una piedra en la cabeza como si
llevasen un sol apagado,
la bella en su cueva de estalactitas y el son de sus ajorcas
de escorpiones,
el hombre cubierto de ceniza que adora al falo, al estiércol y
al agua,
los músicos que arrancan chispas a la madrugada y hacen bajar
al suelo la tempestad airosa de la danza,
el collar de centellas, las guirnaldas de electricidad balanceándose
en mitad de la noche.
los niños desvelados que se espulgan a la luz de la luna,
los padres y las madres con sus rebaños familiares y sus bestias
adormecidas y sus dioses pertificados hace mil años,
las mariposas, los buitres, las serpientes, los monos, las vacas, los
insectos parecidos al delirio,
todo este largo día con su terrible cargamento de seres y cosas,
encalla lentamente en el tiempo parado.

Todos vamos cayendo con el día, todos entramos en el túnel,
atravesamos corredores interminables cuyas paredes de aire
sólido se cierran,
nos internamos en nosotros y a cada paso el animal humano
jadea y se desploma,
retrocedemos, vamos hacia atrás, el animal pierde futuro a
cada paso,
y lo erguido y duro y óseo en nosotros al fin cede y cae
pesadamente en la boca madre.
Dentro de mí me apiño, en mí mismo me hacino y al apiñarme
me derramo,
soy lo extendido dilatándose, lo repleto vertiéndose
y llenándose,
no hay vértigo ni espejo ni náusea ante el espejo, no
hay caída,
sólo un estar, un derramado estar, llenos hasta los bordes, todos
a la deriva:
agua vertida, volvemos al principio.

red bougainvillea black through darkness of red, purple in
   accumulated blue,
women bricklayers carrying stones on their heads as if they
   carried extinguished suns,
the beauty in her stalactite cave, the beauty rings with her
   scorpion bangles,
the man covered with ashes who worships the phallus, dung
   and water,
musicians who tear sparks out of daybreak and make the airy
   tempest of the dance come down to earth,
the collar of sparkle, electric garlands in equilibrium
   at midnight,
the sleepless children picking fleas by moonlight,
fathers and mothers with their family flocks and their beasts
   asleep and their gods petrified a thousand years ago,
butterflies, vultures, snakes, monkeys, cows, insects looking
   like madness,
all this long day with its frightful cargo of beings and things
   slowly being stranded on suspended time.

We all go declining with the day, we all enter the tunnel,
we cross through endless galleries whose walls of solid air close
   behind us,
we imprison ourselves in ourselves and at each step the human
   animal pants and topples,
we fall back, we give our ground, the animal loses future at
   each step,
that which is erect and hard and bony in ourselves finally gives
   way, falling heavily into the mother mouth.
Within myself I crowd myself, in my own self I press myself and
   as I crowd myself I overflow,
I am extended and I expand; the full one, spilling and
   filling myself,
there is no vertigo nor mirror nor nausea facing the mirror, there
   is no downfall,
only a being, an overflowing being, full to the brim,
   and adrift:
spilled water, we return to the origin.

la cabeza cae sobre el pecho y el cuerpo cae sobre el cuerpo sin
    encontrar su fin, su cuerpo último,
la noche dobla la cintura, cede el alma, caen racimos de horas,
    cae el hombre
como un sol, caen racimos de astros, como un fruto demasiado
    maduro cae el mundo.

Pantanos del sopor, algas acumuladas, cataratas de abejas sobre
    los ojos mal cerrados,
festín de arena, horas mascadas, imágenes mascadas, vida
    mascada siglos
hasta no ser sino una confusión estática que entre las aguas
    somnolientas sobrenada,
agua de ojos, agua de bocas, agua nupcial y ensimismada,
    agua incestuosa,
agua de dioses, cópula de dioses, agua de astros y reptiles, selvas
    de agua de cuerpos incendiados,
beatitud de lo repleto sobre sí mismo derramándose, no somos,
    no quiero ser
Dios, no quiero ser a tientas, no quiero regresar, soy hombre y el
    hombre es
el hombre, el que saltó al vacío y nada lo sustenta desde entonces
    sino su propio vuelo,   ʼ
el desprendido de su madre, el desterrado, el sin raíces, ni cielo
    ni tierra, sino puente, arco
tendido sobre la nada, en sí mismo anudado, hecho haz, y no
    osbstante partido en dos desde el nacer, peleando
contra su sombra, corriendo siempre tras de sí, disparado,
    exhalado, sin jamás alcanzarse,
no, anclar el ser, asirlo y en roca plantarlo, zocalo
    del relampage...

the head falls on the breast and body falls on body without
  finding its goal, its final body,
night doubles over, the soul gives way, clusters of hours fall,
  man falls
like a sun, clusters of stars fall, like overripe fruit the
  world falls.

Marshes of lethargy, accretions of algae, bees in cataracts over
  half-open eyes,
a feast of sand, hours chewed, images chewed, life
  chewed centuries
with no existence other than ecstatic chaos which floats among
  the sleeping waters,
water of eyes, water of mouths, wedding waters lost in
  contemplation, water of incest,
water of gods, copulation of gods, water of stars and reptiles,
  water-forests of burnt bodies,
beatitude of fullness, overflowing itself, we are not, I do not want
  to be
God, I do not want to grope in the dark, I will not return, I am
  a man and man is
man, he who leapt to the void and since then nothing has
  sustained him but his own wing,   ·
the one who let go of his mother, the exiled, rootless, with neither
  heaven nor earth, a bridge, a bow
stretched over nothing, in himself unified, made whole, and
  nevertheless split from the moment of his birth, struggling
against his shadow, always running behind himself, blundering,
  exhausted, without ever reaching himself,
no, take hold of the being, anchor it, plant it in the rock, base
  of lightning ...

¿No hay salida?

Oigo correr entre bultos adormilados y ceñudos un incesante río.
Es la catarata negra y blanca, las voces, las risas, los gemidos del
mundo confuso, despeñándose.
Y mi pensamiento que galopa y galopa ya no avanza, también
cae y se levanta
y vuelve a despeñarse en las aguas estancadas del lenguaje.
Hace un segundo habría sido fácil coger una palabra y repetirla
una vez y otra vez,
cualquiera de esas frases que decimos a solas en un cuarto sin
espejos
para probarnos que no es cierto,
                              que aún estamos vivos,
pero ahora con manos que no pesan la noche aquieta la furiosa
marea
y una a una desertan las imágenes, una a una las palabras se
cubren el rostro.

Pasó ya el tiempo de esperar la llegada del tiempo, el tiempo de
ayer, hoy y mañana,
ayer es hoy, mañana es hoy, hoy todo es hoy, salió de pronto de
sí mismo y me mira,
no viene del pasado, no va a ninguna parte, hoy está aquí, no es
la muerte
—nadie se muere de la muerte, todos morimos de la vida—, no
es la vida
—fruto instantáneo, vertiginosa y lúcida embriaguez, el vacío
sabor de la muerte de más vida a la vida—,
hoy no es muerte ni vida,
no tiene cuerpo, ni nombre, ni rostro, hoy está aquí,
echado a mis pies, mirándome.

The endless instant

I hear an incessant
   river running between dimly discerned, looming
   forms, drowsy and frowning.
It is the black and white cataract, the voices,
   the laughter, the groans, of a confused
   world hurling itself from a height.
And my thoughts that gallop and gallop and get
   no further also fall and rise, and turn
   back and plunge into the stagnant waters of
   language.
A second ago it would have been easy to grasp a
   word and repeat it once and then again,
any one of those phrases one utters alone in a
   room without mirrors
to prove to oneself that it's not certain,
                  that we are still alive after all,
but now with weightless hands night is lulling the
   furious tide, and one by one images recede,
   one by one words cover their faces.

The time is past already for hoping for time's
   arrival, the time of yesterday, today and tomorrow,
yesterday is today, tomorrow is today, today all
   is today, suddenly it came forth from itself
   and is watching me,
it doesn't come from the past, it is not going
   anywhere, today is here, it is not death—
no one dies of death, everyone dies of life—it
   is not life—instantaneous fruit, vertiginous
   and lucid rapture, the empty taste of death
   gives more life to life—
today is not death nor life,
has no body, nor name, nor face, today is here,
   cast at my feet, looking at me.

Yo estoy de pie, quieto en el centro del círculo que hago al ir
cayendo desde mis pensamientos,
estoy de pie y no tengo adonde volver los ojos, no queda ni una
brizna del pasado,
toda la infancia se la tragó este instante y todo el porvenir son
estos muebles clavados en su sitio,
el ropero con su cara de palo, las sillas alineadas en espera de
nadie,
el rechoncho sillón con los brazos abiertos, obsceno como morir
en su lecho,
el ventilador, insecto engreído, la ventana mentirosa, el presente
sin resquicios,
todo se ha cerrado sobre sí mismo, he vuelto adonde empecé,
todo es hoy y para siempre.

Allá, del otro lado, se extienden las playas inmensas como una
mirada de amor,
allá la noche vestida de agua despliega sus jeroglíficos al alcance
de la mano,
el río entra cantando por el llano dormido y moja las raíces de la
palabra libertad,
allá los cuerpos enlazados se pierden en un bosque de árboles
transparentes,
bajo el follaje del sol caminamos somos dos reflejos que cruzan
sus aceros,
la plata nos tiende puentes para cruzar la noche, las piedras nos
abren paso,
allá tú eres el tatuaje en el pecho del jade caído de la luna, allá
el diamante insomne cede
y en su centro vacío somos el ojo que nunca parpadea y la fijeza
del instante ensimismado en su esplendor.

I am standing, quiet at the center of the circle
   I made in falling away from my thoughts,
I am standing and I have nowhere to turn my eyes
   to, not one splintered fragment of the past
   is left,
all childhood has brought itself to this instant
   and the whole future is these pieces of
   furniture nailed to their places,
the wardrobe with its wooden face, the chairs
   lined up waiting for nobody,
the chubby armchair with its arms spread, obscene
   as if dead in its bed,
the electric fan—conceited insect—the lying
   window, the actual without chinks or cracks,
all has shut itself up in itself, I have come back
   to where I began, everything is today and
   forever.

Way off there, on the other side, shores extend,
   immense as a look of love,
there the night clothed in water displays its
   hieroglyphs within hand's reach,
the river enters singing along the sleeping plain
   and moistens the roots of the word freedom,
there enlaced bodies lose themselves in a forest
   of transparent trees,
under the leaves of the sun we walk, we
   are two reflections that cross swords with
   each other,
silver stretches bridges for us to cross the night,
   stones make way for us,
there you are the tattooing on the jade breast fallen
   from the moon, there the insomniac diamond
   yields
and in its empty center we are the eye that never
   blinks and the transfixion of the instant
   held within itself in its splendor.

Todo está lejos, no hay regreso, los muertos no están muertos,
los vivos no están vivos,
hay un muro, un ojo que es un pozo, todo tira hacia abajo, pesa
el cuerpo,
pesan los pensamientos, todos los años son este minuto desplo-
mándose interminablemente,
aquel cuarto de hotel de San Francisco me salió al paso en
Bangkok, hoy es ayer, mañana es ayer,
la realidad es una escalera que no sube ni baja, no nos movemos,
hoy es hoy, siempre es hoy,
siempre el ruido de los trenes que despedazan cada noche a la
noche,
el rucurrir a las palabras melladas,
la perforación del muro, las idas y venidas, la realidad cerrando
puertas,
poniendo comas, la puntuación del tiempo, todo está lejos, los
muros son enormes,
está a millas de distancia el vaso de agua, tardaré mil años en
recorrer mi cuarto,
qué sonido remoto tiene la palabra vida, no estoy aquí, no hay
aquí, este cuarto está en otra parte,
aquí es ninguna parte, poco a poco me he ido cerrando y no
encuentro salida que no dé a este instante,
este instante soy yo, salí de pronto de mí mismo, no tengo
nombre ni rostro,
yo está aquí, echado a mis pies, mirándome mirándose mirarme
mirado.

Fuera, en los jardines que arrasó el verano, una cigarra se ensaña
contra la noche.
¿Estoy o estuve aquí?

Tokio, 1952

All is far off, there is no way back, the dead
    are not dead, the living are not alive,
there is a wall, an eye that is a well, all that is
    pulls downwards, the body is heavy,
thoughts are heavy, all the years are this minute
    that is dropping interminably down,
from that hotel room in San Francisco I stepped
    right into Bangkok, today is yesterday,
    tomorrow is yesterday,
reality is a staircase going neither up nor down,
    we don't move, today is today, always is today,
always the sound of trains that depart each night
    towards night,
the resort to toothless words,
the boring through of the wall, the comings and
    goings, reality shutting doors,
putting in commas, the punctuation of time, all
    is far off, the walls are enormous,
the glass of water is thousands of miles away, it
    will take me a thousand years to cross my
    room again,
what a remote sound the word life has, I am not
    here, there is no here, this room is some-
    where else, here is nowhere, little by little
    I have been shutting myself and I find no
    exit that doesn't give onto this instant,
this instant is I, I went out of myself all at
    once, I have no name and no face,
I am here, cast at my feet, looking at myself
    looking to see myself seen.

Outside, in the gardens that summer has ravaged
    a cicada rages against the night.
Am I or was I here?

                                                    [D.L.]

El río

La ciudad desvelada circula por mi sangre como una abeja.
Y el avión que traza un gemido en forma de S larga, los tranvías
   que se derrumban en esquinas remotas,
ese árbol cargado de injurias que alguien sacude a medianoche en
   la plaza,
los ruidos que ascienden y estallan y los que se deslizan y
   cuchichean en la oreja un secreto que repta
abren lo oscuro, precipicios de aes y oes, túneles de
   vocales taciturnas,
galerías que recorro con los ojos vendados, el alfabeto somnoliento
   cae en el hoyo como un río de tinta,
y la ciudad va y viene y su cuerpo de piedra se hace añicos al
   llegar a mi sien,
toda la noche, uno a uno, estatua a estatua, fuente a fuente,
   piedra a piedra, toda la noche
sus pedazos se buscan en mi frente, toda la noche la ciudad habla
   dormida por mi boca
y es un discurso y jadeante, un tartamudeo de aguas y piedra
   batallando, su historia.

Detenerse un instante, detener a mi sangre que va y viene, va y
   viene y no dice nada,
sentado sobre mí mismo como el yoguín a la sombra de la
   higuera, como Buda a la orilla del río, detener al instante,
un solo instante, sentado a la orilla del tiempo, borrar mi imagen
   del río que habla dormido y no dice nada y me
   lleva consigo,
sentado a la orilla detener al río, abrir el instante, penetrar por
   sus salas atónitas hasta su centro de agua,
beber en la fuente ser la cascada de sílabas azules que cae de los
   labios de piedra,

The river

The restless city circles in my blood like a bee.
And the plane that traces a querulous moan in a long S, the
    trams that break down on remote corners,
that tree weighted with affronts that someone shakes at midnight
    in the plaza,
the noises that rise and shatter and those that fade away and
    whisper a secret that wriggles in the ear,
they open the darkness, precipices of a's and o's, tunnels of
    taciturn vowels,
galleries I run down blindfolded, the drowsy alphabet falls in the
    pit like a river of ink,
and the city goes and comes and its stone body shatters as it
    arrives at my temple,
all night, one by one, statue by statue, fountain by fountain,
    stone by stone, the whole night long
its shards seek one another in my forehead, all night long the
    city talks in its sleep through my mouth,
a gasping discourse, a stammering of waters and arguing stone,
    its story.

To stop still an instant, to still my blood which goes and comes,
    goes and comes and says nothing.
seated on top of me like a yogi in the shadow of a fig tree, like
    Buddha on the river's edge, to stop the instant,
a single instant, seated on the edge of time, to strike out my
    image of the river that talks in its sleep and says nothing and
    carries me with it,
seated on the bank to stop the river, to unlock the instant, to
    penetrate its astonished rooms reaching the center of water,
to drink at the fountain, to be the cascade of blue syllables falling
    from stone lips,

sentado a la orilla de la noche como Buda a la orilla de sí mismo
    ser el parpadeo del instante,
el incendio y la destrucción y el nacimiento del instante y la
    respiración de la noche fluyendo enorme a la orilla del tiempo,
decir lo que dice el río, larga palabra semejante a labios, larga
    palabra que no acaba nunca,
decir lo que dice el tiempo en duras frases de piedra, en vastos
    ademanes de mar cubriendo mundos.

A mitad del poema me sobrecoge siempre un gran desamparo,
    todo me abandona,
no hay nadie a mi lado, ni siquiera esos ojos que desde atrás
    contemplan lo que escribo,
no hay atrás ni adelante, la pluma se rebela, no hay comienzo ni
    fin, tampoco hay muro que saltar,
es una explanada desierta el poema, lo dicho no está dicho, lo no
    dicho es indecible,
torres, terrazas devastadas, babilonias, un mar de sal negra, un
    reino ciego,
           No,
detenerme, callar, cerrar los ojos hasta que brote de mis párpados
    una espiga, un surtidor de soles,
y el alfabeto ondule largamente bajo el viento del sueño y la
    marea crezca en una ola y la ola rompa el dique,
esperar hasta que el papel se cubra de astros y sea el poema un
    bosque de palabras enlazadas,
           No,
no tengo nada que decir, nadie tiene nada que decir, nada ni
    nadie excepto la sangre,
nada sino este ir y venir de la sangre, este escribir sobre lo escrito
    y repetir la misma palabra en mitad del poema,
sílabas de tiempo, letras rotas, gotas de tinta, sangre que va y
    viene y no dice nada y me lleva consigo.

Y digo mi rostro inclinado sobre el papel y alguien a mi lado
    escribe mientras la sangre va y viene,
y la ciudad va y viene por su sangre, quiere decir algo, el tiempo
    quiere decir algo, la noche quiere decir,

seated on the edge of night like Buddha on his self's edge, to be
the flicker of the lidded instant,
the conflagration and the destruction and the birth of the instant,
the breathing of night rushing enormous at the edge of time,
to say what the river says, a long word resembling lips, a long
word that never ends,
to say what time says in hard sentences of stone, in vast gestures
of sea covering worlds.

In mid-poem a great helplessness overtakes me, everything
abandons me,
there is no one beside me, not even those eyes that gaze from
behind me at what I write,
no one behind or in front of me, the pen mutinies, there is
neither beginning nor end nor even a wall to leap,
the poem is a deserted esplanade, what's said is not said, the
unsaid is unsayable,
towers, devastated terraces, Babylons, a sea of black salt, a blind
kingdom,
        No,
to stop myself, to keep quiet, to close my eyes until a green spike
sprouts from my eyelids, a spurt of suns,
and the alphabet wavers long under the wind of the vision and
the tide rolls into one wave and the wave breaks the dike,
to wait until the paper is covered with stars and the poem a
forest of tangled words,
        No,
I have nothing to say, no one has anything to say, nothing and
nobody except the blood,
nothing except this coming and going of the blood, this writing
over the written, the repetition of the same word in mid-poem,
syllables of time, broken letters, splotches of ink, blood that goes
and comes and says nothing and carries me with it.

And I speak, my beak bent over the paper and someone beside
me writes while the blood goes and comes,
and the city goes and comes through his blood, wants to say
something, time wants to say something, the night wants to speak,

toda la noche el hombre quiere decir una sola palabra, decir al
  fin su discurso hecho de piedras desmoronadas,
y aguzo el oído, quiero oír lo que dice el hombre, repetir lo que
  dice la ciudad a la deriva,
toda la noche las piedras rotas se buscan a tientas en mi frente,
  toda la noche pelea el agua contra la piedra,
las palabras contra la noche, la noche contra la noche, nada
  ilumina el opaco combate,
el choque de las armas no arranca un relámpago a la piedra, una
  chispa a la noche, nadie da tregua,
es un combate a muerte entre inmortales dar marcha atrás, parar
  el río de sangre, el río de tinta,
parar el río de las palabras, remontar la corriente y que la noche
  vuelta sobre sí misma muestre sus entrañas de oro ardiendo,
que el agua muestre su corazón que es un racimo de espejos
  ahogados, un árbol de cristal que el viento desarraiga
(y cada hoja del árbol vuela y centellea y se pierde en una luz
  cruel como se pierden las palabras en la imagen del poeta)
que el tiempo se cierre y sea su herida una cicatriz invisible,
  apenas una delgada línea sobre la piel del mundo,
que las palabras depongan armas y sea el poema una sola palabra
  entretejida, un resplandor implacable que avanza,
y sea el alma el llano después del incendio, el pecho lunar de un
  mar petrificado que no refleja nada
sino la extensión extendida, el espacio acostado sobre sí mismo,
  las alas inmensas desplegadas,
y sea todo como la llama que se esculpe y se hiela en la roca de
  entrañas transparentes,
duro fulgor resuelto ya en cristal y claridad pacífica.

Y el río remonta su curso, repliega sus velas, recoge sus imágenes
  y se interna en sí mismo.

Ginebra, 1953

all night long the man wants to say one single word, to speak his
    discourse at last, made up of moldered stones,
and I whet my hearing, I want to hear what the man says, to
    repeat what the drifting city says,
all night the broken stones seek one another, groping in my
    forehead, all night the water fights the stone,
the words against the night, the night against the night, nothing
    lights up the opaque combat,
the shock of arms does not wrench away a single gleam to the
    stone, one spark to the night, no one grants a respite,
it is a fight to the death between immortals to offer retreat, to
    stop the river of blood, the river of ink,
to stop the river of words, to go back upstream, and that the night
    turn upon itself display its bowels of flaming gold,
and that the water show its heart, a cluster of drowned mirrors,
    a glass tree that the wind uproots
(and every leaf of the tree flutters and glints and is lost in a
    cruel light, as the words of the poet's image are lost),
may time thicken and its wound be an invisible scar, scarcely
    a delicate line upon the skin of the world,
let the words lay down their arms and the poem be one single
    interwoven word, an implacable radiance that advances
and may the soul be the blackened grass after fire, the lunar
    breast of a sea that's turned to stone and reflects nothing
except splayed dimension, expansion, space lying down upon
    itself, spread wings immense,
and may everything be like flame that cuts itself into and freezes
    into the rock of diaphanous bowels,
hard blazing resolved now in crystal, peaceable clarity.

And the river goes back upstream, strikes its sails, picks up its
    images and coils within itself.

                                            [P.B.]

El cántaro roto

La mirada interior se despliega y un mundo de vértigo y llama
nace bajo la frente del que sueña:
soles azules, verdes remolinos, picos de luz que abren astros
como granadas,
tornasol solitario, ojo de oro girando en el centro de una
explanada calcinada,
bosques de cristal de sonido, bosques de ecos y respuestas y
ondas, diálogo de transparencias,
¡viento, galope de agua entre los muros interminables de una
garganta de azabache,
caballo, cometa, cohete que se clava justo en el corazón de la
noche, plumas, surtidores,
plumas, súbito florecer de las antorchas, velas, alas, invasión de
lo blanco,
pájaros de las islas cantando bajo la frente del que sueña!

Abrí los ojos, los alcé hasta el cielo y vi cómo la noche se cubría
de estrellas.
¡Islas vivas, brazaletes de islas llameantes, piedras ardiendo,
respirando, racimos de piedras vivas,
cuánta fuente, qué claridades, qué cabelleras sobre una
espalda oscura,
cuánto río allá arriba, y ese sonar remoto del agua junto al
fuego, de luz contra la sombra!
Harpas, jardines de harpas.

Pero a mi lado no había nadie.
Sólo el llano: cactus, huizaches, piedras enormes que estallan
bajo el sol.

The broken waterjar

The inward look unfolds and a world of vertigo and flame is born
    in the dreamer's brow:
blue suns, green whirlwinds, birdbeaks of light pecking open
    the pomegranate stars,
and the solitary sunflower, a gold eye revolving at the center of a
    burnt slope,
and forests of ringing crystal, forests of echoes and answers and
    waves, a dialogue of transparencies,
and the wind, and the gallop of water between the interminable
    walls of a jet throat,
and the horse, the comet, the skyrocket piercing the night's
    heart, and feathers and fountains,
feathers, a sudden blossoming of torches, candles, wings, an
    invasion of whiteness,
birds of the islands singing in the dreamer's brow!

I opened my eyes, looked up at the sky, and saw how the night
    was covered with stars:
living islands, bracelets of flaming islands, burning and breathing
    stones, clusters of living stones,
and all those fountains and clear lights, those long locks against
    a dark shoulder,
and so many rivers, and the far-off sound of water next to fire, of
    light against shadow!
Harps, gardens of harps.

But I was alone in the field:
it was cactus, and thorns, and great rocks cracking in
    the sun.

No cantaba el grillo,
había un vago olor a cal y semillas quemadas,
las calles del poblado eran arroyos secos
y el aire se habría roto en mil pedazos si alguien hubiese gritado:
  ¿quién vive?
Cerros pelados, volcán frío, piedra y jadeo bajo tanto esplendor,
  sequía, sabor de polvo,
rumor de pies descalzos sobre el polvo, ¡y el pirú en medio del
  llano como un surtidor petrificado!

Dime, sequía, dime, tierra quemada, tierra de huesos remolidos,
  dime, luna agónica,
¿no hay agua,
hay sólo sangre, sólo hay polvo, sólo pisadas de pies desnudos
  sobre la espina,
sólo andrajos y comida de insectos y sopor bajo el mediodía
  impío como un cacique de oro?
¿No hay relinchos de caballos a la orilla del río, entre las grandes
  piedras redondas y relucientes,
en el remanso, bajo la luz verde de las hojas y los gritos de los
  hombres y las mujeres bañándose al alba?
El dios-maíz, el dios-flor, el dios-agua, el dios-sangre,
  la Virgen,
¿todos se han muerto, se han ido, cántaros rotos al borde de la
  fuente cegada?
¿Sólo está vivo el sapo,
sólo reluce y brilla en la noche de México
  el sapo verduzco,
sólo el cacique gordo de Cempoala es inmortal?

Tendido al pie divino árbol de jade regado con sangre, mientras
  dos esclavos jóvenes lo abanican,
en los días de las grandes procesiones al frente del pueblo,
  apoyado en la cruz: arma y bastón,
en traje de batalla, el esculpido rostro de sílex aspirando como un
  incienso precioso el humo de los fusilamientos,
los fines de semana en su casa blindada junto al mar, al lado de
  su querida cubierta de joyas de gas neón,
¿sólo el sapo es inmortal?

The crickets were silent.
There was a stray odor of lime and burnt seeds,
the village streets were dry gullies,
and the air would have shattered into a thousand pieces if
    someone had shouted: Who goes there?
Bare hills, a cold volcano, stone and a sound of panting under
    such splendor, and drouth, the taste of dust,
the rustle of bare feet in the dust, and one tall tree in the middle
    of the field like a petrified fountain!

Tell me, drouth, tell me, burnt earth, earth of ground bones, tell
    me, agonized moon:
is there no water,
is there only blood, only dust, only naked footsteps on
    the thorns,
only rags and food for insects and stupor under the impious noon,
    that golden chief?
Are there no horses neighing at the riverbank among the great
    smooth glistening boulders,
in the still water, under the green light of the leaves and the
    shouts of the men and women bathing at dawn?
Where are the gods, the corn-god, the flower-god, the water-god,
    the blood-god, the Virgin,
have they all died, have they all departed, broken waterjars at
    the edge of the blocked fount?
Is only the toad alive?
Does only the gray-green toad glow and shine in the
    Mexican night?
Is only the fat chief of Cempoala immortal?

Is only the toad alive,
reclining under the divine tree of jade which is watered with
    blood, while two young slaves fan him,
leading the great public processions, leaning on the cross:
    weapon and walkingstick,
in battle dress, in a carved stone mask, breathing the smoke of
    the firing squads like a precious incense,
or spending long weekends in his fortified house at the seashore
    with his mistress and her neon jewels?

He aquí a la rabia verde y fría y a su cola de navajas y
 vidrio cortado,
he aquí al perro y a su aullido sarnoso,
al maguey taciturno, al nopal y al candelabro erizados, he aquí
 a la flor que sangra y hace sangrar,
la flor de inexorable y tajante geometría como un delicado
 instrumento de tortura,
he aquí a la noche de dientes largos y mirada filosa, la noche
 que desuella con un pedernal invisible,
oye a los dientes chocar uno contra otro,
oye a los huesos machacando a los huesos,
al tambor de piel humana golpeado por el fémur,
al tambor del pecho golpeado por el talón rabioso,
al tam-tam de los tímpanos golpeados por el sol delirante,
he aquí al polvo que se levanta como un rey amarillo y todo lo
 descuaja y danza solitario y se derrumba
como un árbol al que de pronto se le han secado las raíces, como
 una torre que cae de un solo tajo,
he aquí al hombre que cae y se levanta y come polvo y se arrastra,
al insecto humano que perfora la piedra y perfora los sigleos y
 carcome la luz,
he aquí a la piedra rota, al hombre roto, a la luz rota.

¿Abrir los ojos o cerrarlos, todo es igual?
Castillos interiores que incendia el pensamiento porque otro más
 puro se levante, sólo fulgor y llama,
semilla de la imagen que crece hasta ser árbol y hace estallar
 el cráneo,
palabra que busca unos labios que la digan,
sobre la antigua fuente humana cayeron grandes piedras,
hay siglos de piedras, años de losas, minutos espesores sobre la
 fuente humana.

Dime, sequía, piedra pulida por el tiempo sin dientes, por el
 hambre sin dientes,
polvo molido por dientes que son siglos, por siglos que
 son hambres,
dime, cántaro roto caído en el polvo, dime,

Look at the cold green rage with its tail of knives and
    cut glass,
look at the dog with the mangy howl,
the taciturn maguey, the bristling cactus, the flower that bleeds
    and lets blood,
the flower whose sharp inexorable geometry is like a delicate
    instrument of torture,
look at the night with its long teeth and slashing eyes, the night
    that flays with an invisible stone,
listen to the teeth colliding,
listen to the bones crushing bones,
the thighbone pounding the drum of human skin,
the furious heel pounding the drum of the breast,
the delirious sun pounding the tom-tom of the eardrums,
look at the dust that rises like a yellow king and uproots
    everything and dances alone and falls down
like a tree whose roots have suddenly dried up, like a tower
    collapsing at the first blow,
look at the man who falls and rises and eats dust and crawls along,
the human insect who pierces the rock and pierces the centuries
    and gnashes at the light,
look at the broken rock, the broken man, the broken light.

Is it all the same if we open our eyes or close them?
Thought burns down our interior castles so that another may
    rise in their place, all flame and refulgence,
the seed of an image growing up into a tree that cracks
    the skull,
the word seeking lips that will speak it.
Great stones have cumbered the ancient human fount,
there are centuries of stones, years of flagstones, ponderous stone
    minutes heaped over the human fount.

Tell me, drouth, stone polished smooth by toothless time, by
    toothless hunger,
dust ground to dust by teeth that are centuries, by centuries
    that are hunger,
tell me, broken waterjar in the dust, tell me,

¿ la luz nace frotando hueso contra hueso, hombre contra hombre,
    hambre contra hambre,
hasta que surja al fin la chispa, el grito, la palabra,
hasta que brote al fin el agua y crezca el árbol de anchas hojas
    de turquesa ?

Hay que dormir con los ojos abiertos, hay que soñar con
    las manos,
soñemos sueños activos de río buscando su cauce, sueños de sol
    soñando sus mundos,
hay que soñar en voz alta, hay que cantar hasta que el canto
    eche raíces, tronco, ramas, pájaros, astros,
cantar hasta que el sueño engendre y brote del costado del
    dormido la espiga roja de la resurrección,
el agua de la mujer, el manantial para beber y mirarse y recono-
    cerse y recobrarse,
el manantial para saberse hombre, el agua que habla a solas en la
    noche y nos llama con nuestro nombre,
el manantial de las palabras para decir yo, tú, él, nosotros, bajo
    el gran árbol viviente estatua de la lluvia,
para decir los pronombres hermosos y reconocernos y ser fieles a
    nuestros nombres
hay que soñar hacia atrás, hacia la fuente, hay que remar
    siglos arriba,
más allá de la infancia, más allá del comienzo, más allá de las
    aguas del bautismo,
echar abajo las paredes entre el hombre y el hombre, juntar de
    nuevo lo que fue separado,
vida y muerte no son mundos contrarios, somos un solo tallo
    con dos flores gemelas,
hay que desenterrar la palabra perdida, soñar hacia dentro y
    también hacia afuera,
descifrar el tatuaje de la noche y mirar cara a cara al mediodía y
    arrancarle su máscara,
bañarse en luz solar y comer los frutos nocturnos, deletrear la
    escritura del astro y la del río,
recordar lo que dicen la sangre y la marea, la tierra y el cuerpo,
    volver al punto de partida,

is the light born to rub bone against bone, man against man, hunger
    against hunger,
till the spark, the cry, the word spurts forth at last,
till the water flows and the tree with wide turquoise leaves arises
    at last?

We must sleep with open eyes, we must dream with
    our hands,
we must dream the dreams of a river seeking its course, of the
    sun dreaming its worlds,
we must dream aloud, we must sing till the song puts forth roots,
    trunk, branches, birds, stars,
we must sing till the dream engenders in the sleeper's flank the
    red wheat-ear of resurrection,
the womanly water, the spring at which we may drink and
    recognize ourselves and recover,
the spring that tells us we are men, the water that speaks alone in
    the night and calls us by name,
the spring of words that say I, you, he, we, under the great tree,
    the living statue of the rain,
where we pronounce the beautiful pronouns, knowing ourselves
    and keeping faith with our names,
we must dream backwards, toward the source, we must row back
    up the centuries,
beyond infancy, beyond the beginning, beyond the waters
    of baptism,
we must break down the walls between man and man, reunite
    what has been sundered,
life and death are not opposite worlds, we are one stem with
    twin flowers,
we must find the lost word, dream inwardly and
    also outwardly,
decipher the night's tattooing and look face to face at the
    noonday and tear off its mask,
bathe in the light of the sun and eat the night's fruit and spell
    out the writings of stars and rivers,
and remember what the blood, the tides, the earth, and the body
    say, and return to the point of departure,

ni adentro ni afuera, ni arriba ni abajo, al cruce de caminos,
   adonde empiezan los caminos,
porque la luz canta con un rumor de agua, con un rumor de
   follaje canta el agua
y el alba está cargada de frutos, el día y la noche reconciliados
   fluyen como un río manso,
el día y la noche se acarician largamente como un hombre y una
   mujer enamorados,
como un solo río interminable bajo arcos de siglos fluyen las
   estaciones y los hombres,
hacia, allá, al centro vivo del origen, más allá de fin
   y comienzo.

México, 1955

neither inside nor outside, neither up nor down, at the crossroads
    where all roads begin,
for the light is singing with a sound of water, the water with a
    sound of leaves,
the dawn is heavy with fruit, the day and the night flow together
    in reconciliation like a calm river,
the day and the night caress each other like a man and woman
    in love,
and the seasons and all mankind are flowing under the arches of
    the centuries like one endless river
toward the living center of origin, beyond the end and
    the beginning.

[L.K.]